Jack,

Keep being
entrepreneur & tell

Look forward
Continue to grow.

Happy Birthday!

Wealthology

The Study of Wealth Creation

AmirAnzur.com *@ London.*

1. Introduction

An average American earns USD 63,206 per year, while an average Pakistani earns USD 1,188. You can hire a fresh university graduate in Peshawar, Pakistan, for USD 150 per month, while it will cost you USD 2,700 to hire a similar graduate in London, UK.

Why is there such a difference in wealth? And how can you create even more wealth for yourself quicker as the world moves online?

I am writing this book as it has been a quest for over 20 years of my life to figure out how to create wealth for myself and help others do the same. I am by no means the wealthiest person in the world, but I am towards the top end of wealth creation.

I am a first-generation immigrant to the United Kingdom with an origin from Pakistan. This is the story of how I have helped thousands of people create substantial wealth for themselves.

I see it as my duty to help others along the journey. Now that I am 45 years old and have been actively chasing wealth since I was 21 years old, I thought I would share my key learnings and save you some time and effort and help you enjoy the journey to get there faster.

Just purely by accident of birth, I was given the privilege of travelling around the world and spending time with some of the world's wealthiest people, including several billionaires.

By the end of reading this book, I want you to have a better idea of what wealth is in terms of money and other aspects of life. I want to awaken you to other ideas of how the world outside lives.

There will be parts you don't agree with me with. That is fine. Remember that just because it is written in a book does not mean that it is the truth. Do your own research. Dig around and you may find your own destiny.

So why have I written this book? An average American makes over 53 times what an average Pakistani makes. This always bothered me and having grown up in international schools, I saw that the country I represented was usually at the bottom of the GDP per capita earnings.

Why are immigrants from countries like Pakistan and Afghanistan looking to emigrate to the US, Canada, UK and Australia rather than the other way around?

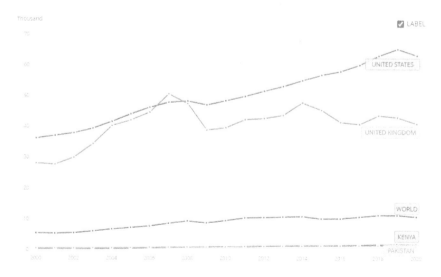

Figure 1-1: GDP Per Capita, Source: World Bank.

Why will the next Mark Zuckerberg more likely not be based in Peshawar rather than Silicon Valley - after all, computers are in both countries?

My true goal is to spread the message of wealth creation and how we can make a wealthier world quicker than at any other time in history. Some of these answers might seem obvious to you, but it took me a long time to develop my own theories after many years of travel and work.

As the world starts to recover from the coronavirus and the destruction of millions of jobs, you might also be wondering what the future holds for you in the post-pandemic world? You might not have anything to do with computers, but can you really get involved and earn an income online too? Or is it too late for you?

I believe that most people are never truly taught about wealth creation and what money is. It determines a lot about your quality of life, but it isn't a subject that is taught in schools. I am not saying that I have all the answers, but I do have many questions that I would like for you to think about and discuss in your classes. You learn history, geography, mathematics and English, so shouldn't making money and creating assets be also crucial in your life?

And as a lot of my readers will already be successful business owners, I teach about how to take your success to the next level using the digital world.

A primary reason I wrote this book is because of a picture I took over a decade ago. It was taken in F10, Islamabad, Pakistan. One of the wealthiest neighbourhoods in Pakistan.

Even though poverty was hidden there, I spotted these kids rummaging through the garbage, trying to make their way in life. As I am now considered one of the "elders" in most parts of the world, I see it as our duty to figure out how to end poverty sooner rather than later. And as a computer scientist, I know that we have this immense opportunity to improve lives worldwide faster than at any other point in history.

Figure 1-2: Not everyone has had the same start in life as you have had.

I have had an adventure, both learning wealth creation for myself and then teaching others how to do it. I hope this book also gives you some solutions to your wealth creation journey - whether you be looking to make your next thousand, million or billion dollars.

2. Confidence is Everything

The first lesson I learned from hanging out with rich people is that confidence is everything. From the age of 8 to 18, I went to the International School of Brussels, Belgium. This school had a tuition fee of USD 50,000 per year, so only a particular class of people went there.

What I saw at the school was that there were so many extra-curricular activities on offer. Student council, yearbook, volleyball, basketball, rugby, baseball, American football, and school newspaper were just some of the activities I took part in. For sports we used to play teams around Europe so on the weekend I got to travel with my teammates to places like Paris, Frankfurt and Cairo. Team members from the opposing team would host us, and we would do the same when they visited us.

This often meant that I would experience Japanese culture while visiting Paris as my host would be a Japanese student and his family studying at the International School of Paris. The point of all these activities was to build our confidence. The more experience you get, the more your confidence grows.

In my junior year, I ran for student council president of the high school with a friend. We lost severely and had one of the most embarrassing speeches in front of the whole school – all our jokes died in front of the crowd.

The following year I asked the same friend if he wanted to run again as I was sure we had a better chance of winning the following year. He declined and said the pain was too much from running the first time. So, I picked another running mate, and we won with a landslide this time.

Two things were different. My confidence was much higher as the other people running for president did it for the first time (usually, only seniors ran for president). And having gone through the pain already, I was able to craft a better marketing strategy by learning from our past lessons – an advantage the others did not have.

The biggest thing you can learn from school is gaining your self-confidence; if you have that, everything else is figureoutable. If you have self-confidence, you will feel more empowered to ask more questions and get the information you need to reach your goals. You will move faster in your business or dream as you won't spend time questioning and doubting yourself.

My biggest regret from my past 20 years of chasing wealth is how often I doubted myself. I have wasted years on self-doubt. I would post an ad on Facebook, get one negative comment, and stop posting ads. Or a family member would shoot down my business idea, and I would stop pursuing it before I let the market decide whether it was a good idea or not.

Even as I write this book, self-doubt enters my mind about whether it will be liked or not. If I did not have the self-confidence, then I would never publish it. If I have gotten you to read this far, it means that I somehow overcame my self-doubts, got the courage to complete it and then actually somehow marketed it to you so you would read it. All this isn't easy if my confidence was not there.

If you want to get to your end goals faster, increase your self-confidence. There are several ways to do this. First, put yourself out of your comfort zone. If, for instance, speaking up and asking a question is something you would never do, try doing it once. The next time it won't feel as difficult. One trick I learned in a standup comedy course I took to increase your confidence was to ask anything even if it is to put down the window of the classroom. This gets easier with time.

Participate in activities and meet different people from around the world rather than staying in the comfort of the friends you already know. When you meet more people you will see that even those that seem weird or different initially are more similar to you than you thought. Travel the world. Or if you can't afford global travel, then travel your country or city. Exploring different places and having adventures like losing your passport or having your wallet stolen will help you build your confidence over time.

Try travelling alone. I often see people travel in groups with their friends and so they have a support for company. It might as well be that they didn't travel at all as they don't get to interact with the locals as they might have done if they were alone. Going to the movies alone shouldn't be embarrassing – travelling alone will build your confidence faster than travelling with friends. Try to pick up the local language when you do it too. I had one friend visit me from the United States who wanted to visit every Hard Rock café in Europe – learn to go where the locals go, not necessarily where you are familiar with.

I also noticed in Pakistani society where there are servants and employers – the key difference is that the servants are taught to have less confidence than their employers. When I moved to Pakistan for a few years I was able to coach a few servants into gaining their confidence and within a few years they had found a way to quit their dead-end jobs paying less then USD 100 per month to starting their own businesses and earning over USD 1,000 per month.

Although my initial hypothesis was that I would teach these servants about making money on the Internet through the likes of facebook, it turned out that this did not work. Often I would ask a servant what his dream was. I would hear back things like "to become a chauffeur". So I would teach them to drive a car. Some of these servants went on to start businesses in the physical world such as a small retail store. Their income and future prospects sky rocketed as they started with one location then grew their store sizes and locations. No formal qualifications. They didn't take classes on retail or read books like I would have done. They just went out and did it. They needed someone to believe in them and give them the confidence. This is what rich kid schools do. They believe in you and give you the confidence to believe in yourself.

One bad teacher can severely limit someone's confidence and I can't even tell you about all the people I have met in my life in their 40s or 50s telling me about how teacher X said they were poor in maths at age 12 and so they never got the hang of it. And if this happened to you, learn to let go and get your confidence back into whatever you want and know that everything is teachable and learnable.

There is a saying for students going to Harvard University – "diamonds in, diamonds out". Meaning that the fact that you got into Harvard is probably a bigger factor of your success than what Harvard actually teaches you. Your confidence and self-esteem go up by attending a top tier school in your city or country and this in turn leads you to try more and accomplish more. You can be a diamond without going to Harvard.

I have also been able to coach people working in the corporate sector and one of the key things that I am able to provide them is simply the confidence in themselves to go make their business or venture a reality. They are often successful making money for their employers but feel bound by the money and perks they are getting – what I am able to do with some of them is to make them believe in their vision and help them strategize the best way of getting out of the rat race.

I used to think that to create wealth everyone should become an entrepreneur but now I don't agree with this. Truth is becoming an entrepreneur is hard work. Really hard work. I have had to sacrifice family time, friendships and being out of the loop of what normal media shows us about life in order to pursue my wealth creation journey. Wealth creation does not need to be difficult or stressful.

In fact what I have learned is how much of a mind game wealth creation is. You don't need to be a millionaire or a billionaire to be happy. There are very few people that come to billionaire status, but confidence while being able to handle debt or not knowing how you will pay your next rent will make you much happier.

Once you have your confidence, the other steps to wealth creation will become easier. This is good news even if you don't have the right education or didn't have the ideal childhood. As once you get the confidence you can learn what you need and grow your wealth to whatever you limit yourself to. I am not saying it is going to be easy. You might spend a few years in a smaller house than your other corporate working friends but just having the belief in yourself will mean that your life will be full of passion and you will enjoy getting up and working through the problems that will inevitably appear on your journey to success.

Figure 2-1: Confidence is everything.

3. Your Greatest Asset

Your greatest asset is your time. It is the one thing you can never get back. All of us have exactly the same amount of time in the day. Bill Gates. Elon Musk. The beggar you met on the street. The banker. The consultant. The lawyer.

You must guard your time. It is more important than the Ferrari you own or the big house in the fancy neighbourhood that you can buy. If you are in a job you hate, you are destroying your soul. Figure out how to get out of it. Work the evenings and the weekends on your ideas and figuring out how you will earn an income for yourself.

Come up with hypothesis for products and services that you can sell and go test these out. If entrepreneurship is not for you then get another job that you will be happier in – even if it pays you less money.

You will never get back your time. And you know who is now trying to suck as much time out of you as possible? Facebook. YouTube. LinkedIn. Instagram. SnapChat. TikTok.

There are ways that you can use these social media platforms to make money but for 99 % of people, they will waste their time – or at least they will be entertained (even that is doubtful as many studies show a link between depression and social media) – but they won't make money. No one pays you to consume content. They pay you to create content.

I have had to train myself to focus. I had to exit a few WhatsApp groups. Just as anyone who is trying to get in shape tries to avoid the bakery, as I try and increase my wealth, I avoid going on platforms like facebook. The only way I can increase my wealth is to spend time writing my book or creating software or some other sorts of ideas or meeting people to sell something to. I use facebook for paid promotions and advertising but not really for keeping friends updated as that consumes a lot of time (my ego wants to keep checking to see how many likes I got).

You need to guard your time and train your brain to focus – this will be hard at first but it is just like going to the gym. You need to develop better focus habits and focus is a muscle just like any other muscle.

You may also have to attend less social gatherings with your friends and family. One reason I was able to increase my wealth substantially by living in London is that I have less family around me. If I was in a place like Islamabad, Pakistan where I have many uncles and family, I would be obligated to go to weddings, funerals, birthday parties or otherwise people might get upset. But you need to let them know that you are busy for a few months/years as you need focus time.

Get as much uninterrupted time as possible. I have a home studio away from my immediate family (but close by) as well as away from my offices and employees. This gives me time to focus. I can use this time to learn things online or read books. Or create products like this one. Or talk to potential clients, suppliers and partners. This is one of the reasons I don't even take co-working spaces like WeWork as I need that alone time to focus.

If you are leading your company, you might have an office nearby for your employees, but try getting a room or a separate office or apartment somewhere else for yourself. This way you won't get interrupted. Turn off your notifications on your phone or laptop so you can go for a while without taking away your attention.

Your attention is your asset. Remember that money is simply a number in a database. You could be USD 100,000 in debt or have a million dollars in your bank account but that is simply a number in a database. Your attention is what will cause you to grow or lose your money.

The television and newspapers will use tricks like "breaking news" and large font headlines to try to get your attention. But remember you are wiser than to fall for it from now on. Discussing politics and religion will also unlikely get you to substantially increase your wealth.

There are few people that can be "converted" to your point of view – chances are people born in a certain religion will die with the same religion. There are many years of brainwashing that happens to a child when they grow in a certain culture, religion, political belief or even supporting a sports team which are hard to change so it usually isn't worth it for you to spend your time doing that unless you feel that this means more to you than financial wealth.

Entering politics means that there can only be one winner. If person X is president than person Y lost. This could mean that you spend your life pursuing a dream that very few people make – at any one time in the world there are around 200 country heads in the world. They tend to stay there at least 3 years so there is limited opportunity. The world of wealth creation and entrepreneurship though is infinite. Even if I have another company beating me in some product or service, I can go create another product or service.

You don't even have to stay in your own lane when it comes to wealth creation. Just because you studied to become a dentist doesn't mean that you have to be a dentist your whole life. You could open a café or start a software company. Especially in the digital age where you can teach yourself almost anything and hire people from almost anywhere, the restrictions that existed in the last century are not as profound as they are now.

Taking care of an elderly parent might for instance decrease your financial wealth but it gives you other emotional and spiritual benefits. I have seen that different cultures value making money differently. In many families and cultures it is a higher calling to cater to supporting the family or fulfilling cultural/religious obligations than it is to focus on increasing a number in a bank account.

Just as Pakistanis might be spending time and attention on religion and family, in the UK and US people are spending time in pubs and watching football. They are getting drunk and having hangovers the next day (obviously I am over-generalising). Very few are discussing business while at the pub. If you enjoy going to the pub or spending your time on religious duties then go do it – but just be aware that this attention is taking you away from wealth creation.

It is not my place to advice you on how you should lead your life – my concern is around wealth creation. I am just letting you know to consciously choose what you sacrifice.

You might decide that you would rather spend 90 minutes watching a football game, than in working on your business to generate wealth. But also remember it is not only the 90 minutes of play time, but it is also the fact it takes you away from your focus. You need to decide how badly you want it.

When I coach people to become successful entrepreneurs, I teach them to think like Olympic athletes. Every hour needs to be counted. The harder they work, the quicker they achieve their goals. Take a few minutes to list all of your habits (cultural, religious, family etc) that encourage you to either create wealth or those that take away time from you to create wealth.

Which habits do you want to modify?

4. Your Second Greatest Asset

Your second greatest asset is your story. This is firstly the story you tell yourself. The story might be "poor me, I am so unlucky". Or "I didn't have the right parents". Or "why am I so ugly". Or "if I was only taller I would be happier". Or "most startups fail".

These are all stories that you have been telling yourself over the years. You need to bring them from the unconscious mind to the conscious mind so you know what you are dealing with.

It is never too late to have a happy childhood. Many of us reflect back and say that some trauma happened in life that messed up everything but you can also see that everything served a purpose.

I struggled for many years as an entrepreneur and thought maybe I just didn't have it within me. Maybe it wasn't meant to be for me. I didn't have the charisma of Steve Jobs. I didn't live in Silicon Valley. I wasn't a University dropout but had gone the traditional route of academics instead, and maybe this was actually a weakness of mine.

Maybe I didn't deserve to be happy. These were my disempowering stories.

When I figured out all the stories I was telling myself, I began to get results. I didn't call up potential clients thinking that they wouldn't buy my product or service but instead called them believing that what I had to offer was going to be a game-changer for them. That I could help them. That they needed me even more than I needed them.

I used to tell myself that they couldn't afford to pay me but I discovered that many had the money, but I simply didn't know how to ask for it. I started to value my time. If they weren't ready to pay, then I wouldn't be giving them free advice. For those that couldn't afford it or didn't want to invest, they could read my books or just simply not achieve their goals as fast as they could if they hired me.

You also need to tell yourself more empowering stories. Why your clients need you and how you transform their lives. As an example I had a prospective client in his 70s that is a multi-millionaire. I thought he would simply leave his money in the bank account, whereas he could spend some of it with me, and I could help him bring his book to life and help him leave a legacy behind for his children, grandchildren and even great-grandchildren. The money sitting in a bank account will disappear, but his book can influence generations.

You aren't too old to start your business. Or too young. Or that because you have kids, you can't follow your dream. We are here only for a short amount of time; you need to make the most out of that time and not spend time on disempowering stories.

I have been low in my journey. I have had suicidal thoughts and even called the Samaritans when I thought there was no way out. I have been broke. Dumped. Fired. And none of these things in retrospect, were as bad as they seemed at the time. Sure, they bruised my ego, but that's it. You don't need to let it hurt you.

The best use of imagination is creativity. The worst use of imagination is anxiety. Use your imagination to create better stories.

Your stories also help you in business. You can give examples to your clients and prospects on how you helped people. Or as a teacher, they can help you teach better as you have better stories.

I teach my students how to embed stories in their books and their sales pitches so that they convert more of their prospects into clients. Your story makes you unique and can be your greatest asset. David Goggins wrote his book "Can't hurt me" and made millions from the back of telling his story, as have many authors throughout history have done.

Remember that holiday trip where you got locked out of your car? Well, it might have seemed like a tragedy at the time, but if you began to look at it as the powerful story it would have added to your life. Your mundane everyday things you will forget, but your stories will stay with you for life.

Your story is your asset. Make it a good one as it doesn't cost anything to change it.

The great thing about everything I have taught so far is that the mindset you bring to life will help you create wealth more than even your connections, inheritance, or education. Many people have all these but don't have the vision or the dream or the story to take their life to the next level. The better the story you can create, the better the influence in the world you can have. And the better the influence in the world, the more wealth you will create.

5. You Are Either Creating or Consuming

You are either creating or consuming content or products and services. As I write this book, I am creating a product. You are at the moment consuming. Consuming can be an investment for the future, but usually, it does not grow your wealth directly.

The newspapers, television, and social media are all competing for you to consume their content. They will have click bait type headlines (e.g. "breaking news" or "you will never believe what J-Lo did") so that you watch or read them. Remember, they are usually making money through advertising, so the more time you spend consuming their content, the more money they make. Therefore, they have an incentive for you to consume their content.

If you want to create wealth, you will have to go towards creation, whether it be to develop software, a physical product or content. If people follow on and consume your product or service, you will make money. If they don't, you won't make money.

The interesting thing about creation is that you will often learn more from creating your own content than from consuming someone else's. As I write this book, I am synthesising years of experience and clarifying my own thinking. I don't know what I am going to write until I have written it.

Start thinking of ways to create more and consume less. Hundreds of years ago, it used to be that you needed to own land to get rich so that farmers could pay you. To get this land, you typically inherited it.

Then in the industrial revolution, to create more wealth, you needed to own factories. And to open a factory, you needed access to capital.

We are now in the knowledge economy. To make money, you simply need ideas and ways of making them happen. Instead of watching Oprah Winfrey, an American billionaire, create wealth through her interviews, you could be creating your own interviews on YouTube. You are not going to get rich watching other people create interviews but you might do so in creating your own content. The usual caveat goes that it is not easy, it takes time, but with time you will get better at producing content and thus building an audience or increasing your wealth.

6. Celebrity Does Not Necessarily Lead to Wealth

I achieved a moderate amount of fame. I was featured in newspapers and television and even did a reality TV show. My lesson learned was that celebrity does not necessarily lead to wealth. In fact, there are a lot of headaches with it. People start thinking that you have a lot of money, and they approach you for money or help.

My inbox would be full of people looking for help in starting their business or helping them find a job or lending them some money for their mother's operation, or even promoting their products or services. I wasn't really prepared for it all. I couldn't say no in the beginning and this led me to spend a lot of time and money helping other people when I myself was not as financially well off as I could have been.

Remember what they teach you on airlines. Before putting the emergency oxygen on your fellow passenger like your child, you must put it on yourself first. So, before you can really help a lot of other people, you must help yourself.

Public Relations and media are still important as they will take your wealth to another level – just think of how much wealth Elon Musk creates for companies just by tweeting about them. Even Microsoft wouldn't have gotten as big as it did unless people knew that the world's richest person, Bill Gates, was associated with the company.

Being a celebrity will lead to you having more status in society, and this leads to becoming more attractive to other men and women. It leads to people wanting to do business with you. The problem I had was I didn't have proper products and services to sell and especially not in the market I was focussed on.

You can build a following and then look to sell them something or advertise to them, but you need to have a strategy in place for your return on celebrity status. Being a celebrity in itself will not lead to wealth, and the celebrities you see on TV or Instagram are not necessarily as rich as you may initially think.

The path to fame is one method of wealth creation but not the only method. Fame can lead to privilege, which might not necessarily have a cash value. For instance, it might be easier for you to get certain meetings if you are famous in your industry or get free products to promote, but fame doesn't necessarily lead to wealth.

I see a lot of people starting political talk shows on YouTube, for instance and this can be a harder niche to cash in on than if you started a podcast on finance for instance where people are more likely to spend money on the products being advertised. You could have a much smaller audience for your finance podcast than your political generic podcast and still make more money.

7. Don't Believe Everything You Read or See

Everyone has their own view of the world and you don't need to believe their view. There are many things that I thought to be true 10 years ago that I no longer believe are true. Just because you read it on a book (including this one) or watched it on television doesn't mean it is true. In this world people are competing for your attention. The way to get more attention is to sensationalize as much as possible and the more extreme position you take the more publicity you can generate.

The more you say something with confidence the more people are likely to believe you. So many people take things which might or might not be true and say them with confidence and convince others to see the world from their point of view.

Even what your parents believe to be true is not necessarily true. Learn to question things. Your patriotism, your political views, your racism, your religion and even the football team you support might be heavily influenced by your parents. You don't have to be restricted by their point of view. See if you could break out of it and see further and better.

Many parents for instance did not grow up in this internet economy so will advise you to get into traditional jobs such as the Government or corporate. They don't have the vision for the new economy that you might do. My business started to really grow when I stopped asking my parents, family and friends for advice on what I should do.

The truth is they hadn't been there. In fact I would actively go out of my way to avoid telling them what I was doing.

Imagine you have option A or option B to go to for your business or wealth creation. If you are thinking option A is the best route but you ask your father and he says you should go with option B then you are defying him and might hurt his feelings so you end up going with option B. Have more faith in yourself and figure out the best route for you. It is better to ask for forgiveness later, than to ask for permission and get rejected.

Your parents might be great doctors and if you want to become a doctor then by all means ask them for career advice but if they are doctors and you want to start podcasting on finance, they might not be the best source for advice.

Especially now on social media there are many people claiming to be experts – often showing their Ferraris and mansions that you should follow or subscribe to them or buy their course. There are many fake videos which are created. Create your own version of reality.

I have learned over time that advice is not universal. Some people say that debt is bad but others would not have been able to create their businesses if it weren't for debt (take real estate and Donald Trump as an example). You can use debt to grow your business but this is also not great advice as this depends on your life situation, you temperament to debt and the industry you are in. Just make sure you do your own research and don't take everything as a given – I have learned this lesson the hard way.

There is literally no barrier to entry in the giving advice business. Everyone has an opinion. If I am not careful, my mother who has never run a tech business and is not really at the forefront of technology, starts giving me advice on how I should run my business. My wife who is 10 years younger than me and also never run a tech business also gives me advice. I have learned to block out those voices or at least limit what I ask them about advice – my mom might be great for cooking advice but running tech businesses is not her thing. My wife is great at design but again running tech businesses is not her thing.

My father was a bureaucrat for his entire career and now in his 70s, so he doesn't have the same risk appetite or entrepreneurial genes that I do in my 40s, and he might also not be the best person to pitch my start-up ideas to. I get his sense of service from him, but not the passion for startups. Love your parents and your spouses, respect everything they have done for you, but create your own path. I listen to my family for how to raise a good family but my business is sacred to me.

One difference I found in hiring Americans rather than Pakistanis was that when I made a job offer to an American they would accept or reject it right away whereas the Pakistani would usually have to come back to me after discussing it with their parents. I often had the extra step of then convincing the parents that joining my startup was a good career move for their son or daughter.

I constantly ask my employees for advice as they know my business side better than most but even then I make up my own mind after listening to their thoughts.

You will also most likely not be surrounded by experts in your field so do go reach out further to find great advice. But the best person to seek advice from is you – not even I could possibly know all the factors to take in when dealing with your situation. One of the first things I say to students who take coaching from me is to not believe everything I say and to make up their own minds – I won't be offended if they don't follow what I advice as I can't possibly know everything to take into account in their circumstances.

What works for Richard Branson or Bill Gates won't necessarily work for you – they are in a completely different situation than you. They have different networks and net worth. You are going to have to step up and take responsibility for your own life and not rely on family, friends, employees, mentors or celebrities.

8. There is Plenty of Room to Innovate

When I first started a software company in the early 2000's I used to be concerned that there was only a limited amount of innovation to be done. Only so many companies could innovate and be the best in my field, which was SMS text messaging at the time. What I learned eventually was there was room for lots of companies in lots of different niches.

Just think about music. A song is typically only 3 minutes long. But how many different types of songs can come into the market and into your head? If anything, the number of songs is growing as the number of musicians that are able to upload their music to platforms like Spotify and YouTube are growing.

Back in the 1980s and 1990s there were limited TV and radio channels like MTV (Music Television) or BBC Radio to limit the number of songs that could be played. Now it is unlimited. Don't fear that you will run out of ideas or ways to innovate. There is an infinite number of ideas out there to go make happen. This should give you some more encouragement that your idea might not be so crazy. Think of yourself as a musician bringing a new song out to market. Let the world hear your music.

You might know that YouTube dominates the market for video, but there are also video sites like Vimeo and Wistia that make millions of dollars targeting different niches that you might not have heard of. They offer different innovations in the same market as YouTube. As sites and ideas grow bigger it is difficult for them to be everything to everybody. That is where you come in and cater to your niche.

Musicians know that not every single song they release will be a hit. Sometimes they cannot predict what the market will like. Think like a musician and let the world listen to your music and decide whether they like it or not. If they like it, you might become the next one hit wonder (which is typically enough) or you might have a more sustained entrepreneurial career like an Elon Musk who has built several ventures.

9. Everything is Figureoutable

Marie Forleo has a great book with the title "Everything is figureoutable". This is a great philosophy to have. If you are broke right now, do not worry you can figure out how to get out of poverty. It may not happen overnight, but it will happen for you if you try enough things.

We are in one of the best times in history. Many decades ago the true way to create wealth was to buy property or to invest in a factory. All these took a large amount of capital or access to capital. In the 2020s and beyond the true wealth will be created by ideas and the execution of those ideas.

Once you have an inkling of an ideas you can figure out things via Google, YouTube or even buying books from Amazon. You can figure everything out.

For my second online business in 2003 I had an idea that you should be able to shop using SMS text messaging (this was before the time of smartphones). I didn't know how I was going to do it, anything about programming or even how SMS technology worked. But through many months of research, teaching myself programming by reading a 1,008 page book (the ways to teach yourself programming are even easier now), learning technical knowledge such as APIs and then figuring out how to connect with a giant retailer like Amazon I was able to figure it out. It began though with a vision of how the world could work. Everything else was figureoutable.

I ended up winning the European prize for innovation, but my real pride was having started with a vague vision and working out the way to get there. Companies like Google,

Intel, Samsung and Xbox were using my platform which I had started and coded from my bedroom in North London. I didn't know anything about sales or how to charge or invoice a customer or setup a company or hire an employee. But I figured it out. Once you do many of these types of ventures, your confidence grows and it enables you to try even more things – of course, you are not always going to be successful, and it may take longer then you initially thought but just starting on the journey will lead you somewhere.

You too should start with a vision – even if it is a vague one – and trust in yourself to figure out everything else along the way.

10.   Short is Better Than Long

The shorter you can make things the better. Remember that people have a lot more distractions than they used to 30 years ago. They want quick fixes and quicker solutions. For instance, this book I will try to make around 100 pages whereas my previous book was three times the length. You can do shorter forms of content.

How quickly can you get your clients to understand what you offer and how you can benefit them? How little of their time can you take? For instance, one of the things I do is to help entrepreneurs and businesspeople bring their non-fiction books out to market. I have had to streamline the benefits so they "get it" and the value of the proposition. I have had to streamline my processes with the ghost writers, editors and cover designers on how to do everything to take less of the client's time.

I help businesses bring their software and apps out to market. This has taken me years of developing a network with developers and understanding the business. Most of my clients are not technical at all and I make the process easy for them through reusing code and creating templates.

People will pay you to save them time. What can you do that will save other people time? Remember they are paying you to solve a problem. If you are a fitness coach, then they will hire you as they know you have done all the research and instead of sending them to read countless books you will give them specific advice to help them get to their fitness goals faster.

Uber saves people time in that instead of having to wait to hail a taxi that is passing by outside, you can simply order one from your phone and wait for it to come to you. Instead of having to take out cash to pay for the cab, you have your credit card linked to the app and it takes the money automatically.

Saving people time will lead you to create wealth for yourself.

11.   The Pyramid of Wealth Creation

What I have discovered over time of coaching both small and large businesses as well as entrepreneurs is the pyramid of wealth creation. At the bottom you have the low skilled jobs. This could be for instance data entry or working as a cashier at a McDonalds.

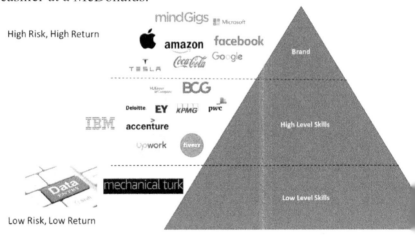

Figure 11-1: The Pyramid of Wealth Creation.

It is relatively easy to get into these jobs as you can quickly be trained. The good thing is that you can start making money from day one.

The downside is unless you really get noticed and have a lot of patience it can take a long time to progress in your wealth creation, that is if you do progress at all.

The middle of the wealth creation is higher skilled jobs. This could be for instance going onto freelancing platforms like fiverr.com or upwork.com. Or even towards the top

end would be working for consulting companies like
Accenture, Deloitte, McKinsey, PWC, BCG or KPMG.

Consultants who become partners at their consulting
companies can earn over USD 1,000,000 per year if they
are working in a developed economy. The way this works
is that if they provide value to corporate clients who have
more money than small businesses, they can charge out a
lot more for their fees. Helping a corporation with USD 1
billion in sales per year increase their revenue by 1 %
means that you increase their sales by USD 10,000,000 and
this is a lot greater than helping a small business earning
USD 100,000 per year increase their revenue by 1 % which
is only USD 1,000. Both take the same amount of
consulting time to help from the consultant, but the bigger
consulting companies typically have the relationships to
help sell to the larger corporates.

I have been in this middle part of the pyramid for a
significant part of my career – beginning with Accenture
and then working for a Big 4 consulting company. I have
also given advice to small entrepreneurs as an independent
consultant. My lesson – the larger the company you can
advise, the more you can earn. For instance, when working
with Google I have made USD 10,000 for a day of my time
as I had a very specialist skill that they needed at the time.

At the top of the wealth pyramid is creating brands. This
has the highest risk as you don't get a salary when you
create a brand. You could end up with nothing or if you are
successful you could end up making a large amount of
income for yourself and for your key employees.

The United States has been traditionally able to create the
greatest brands. Firstly, it had strong intellectual property

rights. You could easily be sued for using the Coca-Cola logo for instance. Secondly, there is a large, rich and homogenous market. Selling to people in New York was relatively similar to selling to people in California. You could start a Starbucks in Seattle and eventually grow the brand to Florida.

Third, there is easy access to capital. You can borrow easily in the United States or get access to investors who will back your ideas. In developing countries like Kenya, Bangladesh or Pakistan, capital is harder to get so there is not as much investment into new ideas.

Creating a brand is not for everyone. It takes time, energy and investment. I used to think how I would ever get employees if I am training people to become entrepreneurs but I realized that often you are better off being employee number 12 in a large brand then you are starting a smaller company by yourself.

When Microsoft floated on the stock exchange, it created over 1,000 millionaires. Companies like Google pay some of their employee's tens of millions of dollars a year. It is hard though to become a billionaire unless you start a brand or at least are an early employee or a CEO of a brand. Susan Wojcicki who became Google's first marketing manager is worth USD 580 million. Early or senior employees at brands can make significant wealth.

It is crucial to learn what makes a great brand and that is where true wealth is created. Working at a great brand is also a great path to wealth creation and can lead to a fulfilling and prosperous life. As there are a lot more brands that exist in a country like United States, there is a

lot more wealth that is created there than most other
countries in the world.

12.   The Simple Wealth Formula

The other formula I have discovered for wealth creation is what I call the Simple Wealth Formula:

Amount of Value You Can Add

x   Number of People You can Impact

-   Number of People Who Can Do What You Do

-   Cost to Serve

=   Total Wealth Created

Basically, you want to increase the value you can add to a client. For instance, I offer a done for you service in which we hire, train and manage resources such as software developers for people looking to bring innovations to market. It basically takes the headache out of hiring, training and managing staff. For this we charge a premium as we feel we add a lot of value.

You will need to figure out how you can help clients in some way. How can you add value to their lives? The great thing now is that you can teach yourself almost anything. For instance, you could go on Udemy.com and take a course on facebook marketing and then open a facebook marketing agency for clients. In the old economy there were many barriers such as getting university degrees – but now you can teach yourself almost anything and start selling it. This is how you create value and make money for yourself.

The second part to the equation is being able to help more people. This is also obvious. The more clients you get, the more you can make. The internet has exploded the wealth creating opportunities in the world as it has allowed more people to connect. Therefore companies were able to create billionaires out of people like Mark Zuckerberg so quickly.

Thirdly, you need to be as unique as possible. In the internet economy it is possible to get copied very quickly so you will need to stay one step ahead of the competition. This is why wealth in America was as big as it has been as there was strong intellectual property rights. This meant that you couldn't be copied as quickly.

Tesla has become the most valuable car company in part because it is much more difficult for other companies to copy the PR factor that Elon Musk, its founder, can generate. SpaceX, another Elon Musk company, is so unique as it has great relationships with the US governments so few people can compete with it for the big government contracts.

Finally, you need to have as low a cost to serve as possible. This is why Nike manufactures in countries like Vietnam and China. They own the brand but make their costs as low as possible to the point that they often got accused of running sweatshops.

Especially due to the post-corona world where people are more used to working remotely, you also need to hire teams remotely. Remember a university graduate from Peshawar, Pakistan will expect USD 150 as a starting salary, while a university graduate from London, UK will expect USD 2,700 per month. I was able to start aartec.com as a digital innovation company as I was able to start with hiring people for USD 150 per month and train them to deliver the same as those in London. It would have been a lot more difficult for me to start my digital innovation agency if I could only hire talent in the West as the initial months when you start you need to pay salaries when you might not have any clients.

Think of a simple wealth formula for you and your industry and how can you create wealth using it.

13.   The Gamification of Life

As a computer scientist I have learned about gamification. Gamifications are little rewards that you can put inside software so that people are more likely to use it. For instance, on Facebook your number of likes and comments are displayed so that the more you post, the more you want to come back to the app to see how many people liked or commented on your post.

In life there is also gamification. In the United States, wealth creation is gamified. For instance, even if you become a billionaire, publications like Forbes will put you on a chart and let you know that there are others ahead of you. If you look online many of those that build a following do so as they flaunt their wealth.

One of the reasons Donald Trump came to power is he showed off his airplanes and mansions and the average American thought that that is how you become successful.

In places like Pakistan, one is taught to be humble. It is considered in bad taste to show off too much – although the same applies at a smaller scale as people want to live in rich neighbourhoods and have big houses. For safety reasons though you might not want to keep a flashy car, even if you could afford it.

American wealth is more open as you can see what people own on the stock market. American wealth is also more distributed as so many people own shares in stocks in companies across America. If you invested USD 1,000 in Amazon stock in 1997 when it first floated on the stock exchange you would have over USD 1,500,000 by 2021. Americans play the stock market game – predicting when prices will go up or down. Not only does Jeff Bezos get rich, but thousands of others create wealth along his journey too.

In other countries gamification can take place in the form of religion where people try to score points to get into heaven. Material wealth is not as important. If you have ever driven a Ferrari, you will know that it is actually trickier to drive than a Toyota but its price is much higher and its prestige is randomly given a higher value in society as society has been gamified in this way.

Having worked with large corporations, I also noticed that they had created better games letting employees know how to get raises and promotions which were aligned to their objectives.

If you want to create substantial wealth for yourself, you will need to learn how to create games. BitCoin is a game that Satoshi Nakamoto created in the form of a currency and made them a billionaire (identity of who the founder or founders is still not confirmed at the time of writing).

Facebook is a game of social media. YouTube has gamified uploading and watching videos. KPMG has gamified the careers of its thousands of employees so they can give advice while earning a decent income for its employees. You too will need to create gamification of how to build and reward your team as well as software that you might create.

Capitalism is a game. There are always new levels you can reach. A bigger house. A newer car. A larger dividend for your stockholders. It is said that your happiness does not substantially increase when you earn over USD 75,000 per year in the United States. Yet so many people chase the next level in the game of capitalism.

I can also say that once I reached this level, my happiness did not substantially increase but I am still driven every day to increase my numbers – not simply because of my ego or the fact that I want more material things – but capitalism is also a track of how many people you have helped and what kind of an impact you have had on their lives.

The true creators of wealth are those that create the games. Mark Zuckerberg for instance has created the game of Facebook. The founders of Airbnb have helped millions of people rent out their spare rooms, but the true wealth creators have been them as they created the game. Start thinking of life in terms of games, figure out the rules and then try to write your own game to wealth.

14.   The 6 and the 9

Figure 14-1: Who is right - the 6 or the 9?

If you lay down a "6" and have two people on either side of it, one will call it a "6" while the other will be convinced that it is a "9". The only way to change the perspective is for one person to go visit the other side.

I grew up with a western approach to money and capitalism. Success was becoming Jeff Bezos or Elon Musk (or in my time Bill Gates and Steve Jobs). When I finally spent a few years in Pakistan in my 30s I saw a different society. Parents would often say that I want my son or daughter to grow up to be a good "Muslim". For me, this didn't necessarily mean that they meant religious, but they wanted them to be a good human being and be caring.

In Britain, which is a relatively secular society, religion has been replaced by football. The only difference is football is monetizable, whereas religion is less so.

When you see football, or most professional sports, you will see the players wearing a sponsored shirt for instance from Samsung. Or being paid to wear Nike shoes. The Brits will go to the pub and pay USD 7 for a pint of beer and drink while watching the game with their friends. They will pay USD 60 to go to the stadium to watch the games.

Just the Premiere League's 20 football club contribute USD 4.6 billion in taxes for the British Government and supports 100,000 jobs.

In Pakistan a lot of socializing happens at the mosque. It is free to attend. Not as many sports are watched aside from the national cricket team so not as much is spent by advertisers.

When I used to advice young students on how to start a business, I was surprised by how many came up with ideas that would improve religious ways of working. For instance, one group were excited by an app that would automatically not allow SMS or calls to your mobile when it was time to pray so you would not be disturbed.

Another young entrepreneur was launching "Bismillah books" and other ventures under the "Bismillah" brand as he said that everyone knew the word Bismillah so it would be familiar to them. But I had to explain that this could be one way of looking at it, the other way was that he could not Trademark the name as it was already in the common domain and if he were to become successful then other people could simply come and copy his ideas and the customers would not know which was his product.

Having travelled a significant amount of the world, I have realized that different societies have different values within them. Even though the Japanese are a relatively rich society they mostly live in small houses. Americans love big houses and big cars. Of course, I am generalising.

The criticism I would sometimes get from my British friends was that Pakistanis would "waste" a lot of time on prayer and other spiritual rituals such as fasting during Ramadan. On the other hand, they would consider it a productive use of time to go to the pub and visit friends or go visit music festivals. These would not necessarily be seen as fun things to do by an average Pakistani.

Every society has their own different ways of seeing the world. Do not judge and assume that your way of seeing the world is the superior way of seeing the world. Some people prioritize family over wealth creation, others prioritize their careers over family. There is no right or wrong way.

As the psychologist Carl Jung says "The shoe that fits one person pinches another, there is no recipe for living that suits all cases". A lot might have to do with where and how you were brought up.

Figure out your own dreams and your own values, not those imposed by your family or your nationality.

15.   Don't Be Afraid to Start Again

Especially in the new economy, you will have many
different careers. An average American now has 14
different jobs in their lifetime and over 4 different careers.
You may take a few steps back, before moving forward.
Don't be afraid to start again.

You might be in your 50s and have been recently laid off
your job or you might be in your 20s and anxious about
what the future holds. Just pick a direction, any direction,
and start moving towards it. You can always change it.
Almost every decision is reversable. Even marriage
doesn't have to be forever.

You will make the best decision you can at the time with
the data you have. Don't beat yourself up for having made
a "bad" decision. Remember that wealth creation is not
simply about the number going into your bank account but
all the connections, skills, knowledge and experiences you
are gathering too.

16.   The Book That Will Change Your Life

The book that will change your life is the one you actually write. As mentioned in the previous chapters you will generate more wealth from creating content than you will from consuming content.

Traditionally it used to be difficult to produce a book. Now, it is easier than at any other time in history. There are print on demand options so that you don't need to order a minimum of 5,000 quantities of books. You don't need a professional publisher deciding if there is enough of a market for your book. You can publish it yourself.

If you follow the major religions almost all were based on books. If you follow successful people that have generated a lot of wealth such as Donald Trump (The Art of the Deal), Richard Branson (Losing my Virginity), Phil Knight – the founder of Nike (Shoe-Dog) all have a book that they brought out to market to talk about their stories.

You might not have the level of financial success that Donald Trump or Richard Branson has but you do have a story.

Your story is an asset just as the number in your bank account is an asset. The more people hear your story, the more they are likely to trust you and do business with you.

You only need to reach your community with your book – you don't need to reach the world. People are often surprised to hear that I have generated over USD 350,000 in business through my first book. The truth is I sold less than a thousand copies and gave away hundreds of copies for free. But at the back of that book, more people wanted to do business with me and hired me a consultant as I was seen as an expert in my niche.

The way I teach book writing is that you can even have a ghost writer write it for you, so you just have to focus on the message. This book isn't about teaching you how to write your book, but I want to let you know that a book can be an asset worth more than your house or your car.

Think about how many millions was generated by Stephen Covey from his book "Seven Habits of Highly Effective People" and even more importantly how many people he was able to reach with his message.

Even if no one reads your book, you will benefit from the process of synthesizing your experience into one place. If writing is not your thing, then you can get your message out through podcasts or YouTube. Just know that your message is an asset and there might be ways to monetize it.

17.   Try More

WHAT IF I FAIL?

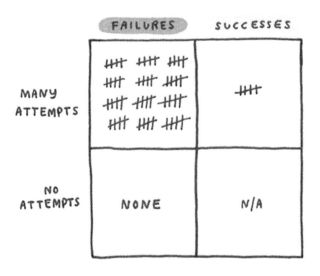

Figure 17-1: The only certain way to fail is to not try.

The more things you try the more you are likely to succeed. And on top of that, the more you are likely to increase your confidence, which will lead you to try even more things.

In this innovation economy those that continue to try more things will be successful. Remember if you are standing still, someone will probably come and overtake you. You need to keep moving. This applies equally to if you are 70 years old or are 15 years old. Or if you have built a billion-dollar company or you are just getting started.

You need to continuously be updating your skills as well. For instance, if you didn't know how to use Zoom when the Covid-19 Virus pandemic hit, you had to learn it pretty quickly use it or you would start getting left out of meetings.

Keep changing your approach until you are successful. Success is not a straight line, there are many curves along the way.

As I mentioned earlier, start with a vague vision which will become clearer over time. You might just find that you achieve more than you even dreamed was possible.

18.   Find Your Why

Simon Sinek in his book "Start with Why" writes that successful companies and people find their Why and that helps them persevere when times get tough. I also eventually found my Why in life and it helped me become more productive. I wanted to help end poverty in Pakistan but after having moved there and realising that it was only making me poor as well, I eventually moved back to the UK.

What I realised was that I could still be of service from outside the country. In fact, I had a skill that fewer people had which was an ability to sell to the global market. This was a lot easier to do from London then it was from Peshawar or Islamabad.

I was not only able to help Pakistanis but started getting students from places like Nepal, Zimbabwe and Kenya. I understood both the needs of the developing world as well as the developed world.

So, I built a digital innovation company called aartec in which you can hire Pakistanis (and eventually others around the world). But we added a twist, we also realized that you needed to train and manage the people that you hired and we could take someone willing to work for a relatively low wage and quickly train them to deliver a high amount of value.

This why has given me juice for many years of my life. I have even had corporate jobs and been able to go to them happily as I know that they were providing me the cash flow to feed my dreams in the evenings and weekends.

To get even more motivation I would visit a poor district of the world every once in a while, so that I would not be too far removed from a dream and forget about the others while I was comfortable in my own home and career.

I would talk to homeless people in London to see what got them on the streets as just hanging out with the wealthy would not necessarily be as inspirational as hanging out with the people that could not necessarily afford your help or repay you in any way.

Your dream could be to entertain people, or to give people better homes to live in. Or to help black people deal with racism or to help poor white people in your neighbourhood or have an impact on climate change or simply to help humanity. Whatever is your why try to find it as that will give you a juicier and more meaningful life.

19. Information and Experiences Are Worth More Than Atoms

You are probably used to seeing people paying a premium price for their Louis Vuitton handbags, Jimmy Choo shoes or their Lamborghinis. Berkin handbags range from USD 12,000 to over USD 200,000. Did you know now in the Information economy virtual products and services are going to be worth more than physical products and services?

I have paid thousands of dollars to buy video courses or coaching services from teachers. These have no physical assets. The only thing I get is time or the transfer of knowledge.

This is mostly what I sell as well. There are no physical goods changing place, but it is virtual assets. Learn that these have more and more value than the physical goods that you are willing to part ways with.

This also means that it is easier to create wealth in the Information economy as all you need to do is to study or gain experience in a certain field. This is up to you to put in the time rather than have the capital inherited from your parents or getting access to the bank. The most valuable asset here is time. If you can give something enough time, you can win in that game.

If you can design or produce the greatest logo and brands you can outsource the production of the products through websites such as Alibaba.com.

Do not be surprised if you are spending more and more of your income on virtual products and services as that is where the future is.

20. The Experience Curve and the Compound Growth

One thing that people don't appreciate in business and in life as much as they should is the experience curve. In business the experience curve looks something like this:

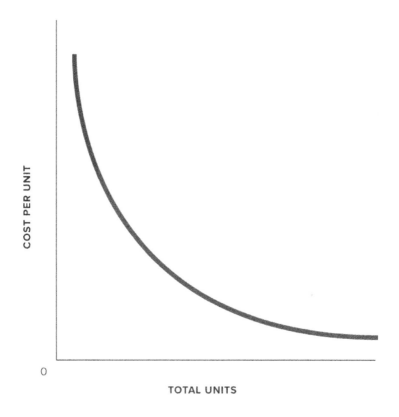

Figure 20-1: The Experience Curve: As you produce more, the cost per unit comes down.

To produce the first unit the cost is very high. You make a lot of mistakes. You are not as efficient as you could be.

The challenge is that most people quit after a few attempts at bringing their product or service out to market. They try a Facebook ad campaign for a week and if it doesn't show any results, they quit.

They try three to five phone calls to pitch their product and if no one buys, they don't think there is a market for their product or service, and they quit. The true rewards are sticking with it and getting better over time.

Every day you should be looking to get better in any way you can. This also gives you the compound growth.

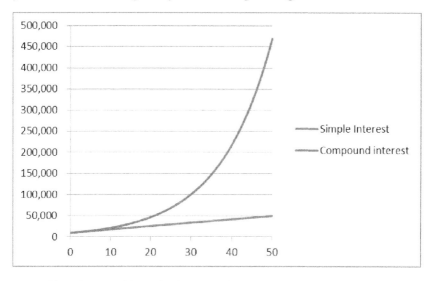

Figure 20-2: Compound Growth will give you big returns over time. Be patient.

At the beginning it is very difficult to create a website or launch a product. Over time it gets easier. When I first started teaching, I didn't know how to help students quickly, now I know and can help them achieve results much faster. This has taken me over 10 years of teaching and 20 years of online businesses. Working every day.

I say I worked every day. But that is a lie. I wasted a lot of months and a lot of years in self-doubt. When things didn't work out or friends and family told me to quit, I listened and went about getting my corporate day jobs. Yes, they were important to help bring the cash flow which allowed me to reinvest in my business ideas but there were many weekends I watched Netflix as I didn't have the confidence that my dream would work for me.

I didn't look at the compound growth for my business.

If you have 1 cent and you double it every day, so for instance it becomes 2 cents in day 2, 4 cents on day 3, 8 cents on day 4, 16 cents on day 5 etc…

You would see something like this:

Day 1	$0.01
Day 2	$0.02
Day 3	$0.04
Day 4	$0.08
Day 5	$0.16
Day 6	$0.32
Day 7	$0.64
Day 8	$1.28
Day 9	$2.56
Day 10	$5.12
Day 11	$10.24
Day 12	$20.48
Day 13	$40.96
Day 14	$81.92
Day 15	$163.84
Day 16	$327.68
Day 17	$655.36
Day 18	$1,310.72
Day 19	$2,621.44

Day 20	$5,242.88
Day 21	$10,485.76
Day 22	$20,971.52
Day 23	$41,943.04
Day 24	$83,886.08
Day 25	$167,772.16
Day 26	$335,544.32
Day 27	$671,088.64
Day 28	$1,342,177.28
Day 29	$2,684,354.56
Day 30	$5,368,709.12
Day 31	$10,737,418.24

So, because of compound growth on the last day of the month you make over five million USD. Whereas all you made on the first day is just a single cent.

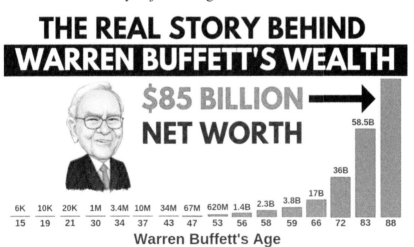

Figure 20-3: Even Warren Buffet took his sweet time to become a billionaire.

Look at Warren Buffett, one of the richest people in the world, and his wealth. He generated billions of dollars in his 80s, whereas he wasn't even a billionaire until his 50s.

It is not just money but contacts, skills, management techniques. They all become easier as you spend time in your craft.

Do not give up hope as much of the progress you will be creating will be invisible – not even you might be able to see it. Keep going and know that you are getting the benefits of the experience curve and the compound effect.

Think about looking at yourself and then going to the gym. After a single workout you are not going to notice a difference. But if you keep doing it and look after 90 days, you will notice a difference. Little changes make a big impact over time.

21. Success Isn't a Straight Line

"Everyone has a plan till they get punched in the face."
Mike Tyson, boxer

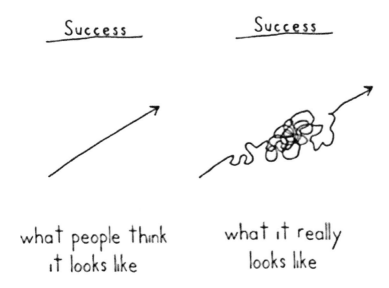

Figure 21-1: The unfortunate truth about success.

There is an illusion that you create a project plan, and you will follow it and become successful. This isn't going to be the case especially in the digital innovation world. You simply don't know what you don't know yet. The more you learn, the more you will change your goals and your ways to get there.

You can't sit and wait and think through all the possibilities you simply have to get going.

Ready. Fire. Aim. If you do it that way then you can adjust the gun after you see where it hit the target.

For me the breakthroughs came when I started pitching products and services to potential clients. I found my digital innovations company as I started meeting people with money and found that many had a need for software services, and I happen to have a network of developers. I undercharged a few projects and maybe over charged for a few before I found the roughly the right prices to charge. Every project made my team and I better at delivery.

It is good to have your 10-year vision but just be flexible on how you get there and just be prepared that it might look different from what you imagined. Remember that the journey is the destination. You need to be chasing a dream or a goal but don't forget to enjoy the squiggly bits of the line to success.

See yourself as successful no matter where you are on the journey. Do not let the lack of academic qualifications, your weight goals, financial success or relationship goals let you feel down. You can be happy where you are. Single. Broke. Overweight. Unqualified.

Some of my happiest times have been when I have had nothing as I was at least going towards something.

Some people are so poor as all they have is money. You have more to offer the world than just the number in your bank account. Yes, money gives you access to resources but creativity can give you access to even more.

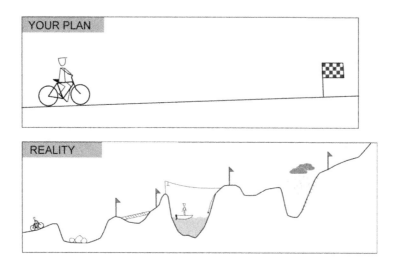

Figure 21-2: The actual path maybe more challenging than your plan.

22.   We are in the Trustonomy

Trust is everything. Some of the customers I have had, I had not done any business with for several years until I finally found a product I could package and sell them that worked for them.

The more trust you can build the faster you can do business. This book is also an asset for me as I am building trust with you while you are reading it. This trust might one day lead to business – either you become a supplier of mine or even better a client of mine.

Social media for all its downsides also has many plus sides. Back in the late 2000's I saw it as a way to spread my message quicker. I have done business before the internet and done door to door selling. I understand how much time it took. In London, I could only really meet two or at most three prospects a day due to the time it took to travel. Now you can engage in dozens of conversations a day thanks to social media.

Look for ways to build trust. This doesn't mean faking it but instead being genuine.

People in general are good. There might be desperate situations where they take off with your money but in general it doesn't happen. Bureaucrats and other non-entrepreneurial people like friends and family will tell you don't trust anyone, but if you want to grow your business you have to have a bit of trust in some people. Most successful entrepreneurs I know are optimistic on people!

23.   Learn to Leap Frog

If you observe frogs, they leap over each other and get further than they would have by jumping by themselves. In business you also need to learn to leapfrog. Someone could have taken years to learn and master their craft, sales, marketing or other techniques.

Figure 23-1: Frogs leaping over each other.

You can come a few years later, look at what they are doing and teach yourself how to do it like they have done it and even do it better. Everything is copyable. Trademarks, patents, copyrights are often broken in the Internet economy as there are too many frogs to try and contain.

Tony Robbins, whom I consider to be one of the greatest life coaches, says that he has people come up to him and say that they are going to be the next Tony Robbins. But he says that they will aim to get to where he is today. Not to where he will be in a years' time.

When I have built software and other services, my content has been copied. There was not much I could do to go after the people that copied, except create better software, products and services.

I used to be quite open about what I was doing. Now, I realise that knowledge is power. I don't teach all my inner work and strategies in the open. I am selective about who I tell what to. Even employees that learn everything from you could setup to become competitors. This doesn't mean that I don't teach my employees to the best of my ability – but simply I am mindful that knowledge is a key asset in business.

I also know that when competitors are copying, I am moving to the next stage. Remember your greatest asset is your brand and your innovation. How difficult do you really think it is to copy Nike? Not that difficult – but Nike remains strong decades after its first launch.

America has become the wealthiest nation as its people are always on its toes innovating and creating better brands to reach more customers. With the gamification of society and stock prices that are visible to the public everyone has a goal of creating more value (e.g., sales) so that the stock goes up and they all have a share of the benefits.

24.   Time and Speed are Critical

Learn to make decisions and act quickly – otherwise you will lose the momentum. If for instance, after having read this book, you feel that I might be able to help you think through your own ideas and reach your goals faster either through software or through life and business coaching then get in touch with me quickly (WhatsApp/SMS/Call +447733003930 or email amir@amiranzur.com) rather than wait for that someday to come around.

Yes, everything has the right time, but just know that your time on this earth is limited and you want to have as much impact as soon as possible. This point really hit me when I hit the age of 45. Now I know people my age that have passed away and I didn't want to leave without having some sort of impact – even if it is just a book. I needed it to be out to as many hands as possible.

In this economy everything can and will be copied. The only way you will stay ahead of the competition is if you learn to run faster. The technology is changing at such a rapid pace that it is impossible to keep up. It is no coincidence that my best developer also works the longest hours. Every hour you work, increases your speed and the pace at which you can deliver.

I am quite old school in my thinking that the harder you work, the more results you will get. Think about an average person who works 40 hours a week. Assuming 48 weeks of work a year that is 1,920 hours per year. Now look at another person giving it 60 hours a week. Assuming 48 weeks of work a year that is a total of 2,880 hours of work a year. This is 960 hours a year more or 24 weeks or 4 months of extra work a year. This adds up the skills, knowledge, connections, sales and earnings over time. Take that over 10 years and you have over 3 years of extra work that someone who works an extra 20 hours does.

I have worked in the corporate consulting sector. Consultants can charge their clients over USD 3,000 a day for their time. What I learned was that they also worked longer hours than those that were not in the consulting industry. Putting in the time will lead to results for you and make you faster and more agile.

25.   Learn to Deal with Stress

If you launch digital or physical assets, stress will enter your life. This might include your websites going down. PayPal freezing your accounts. Employees stealing money from you. You losing the encryption key to the millions of dollars of BitCoins you had bought. Your tenants for a property refusing to vacate and not paying you rent.

The more "stress" you can deal with, the more wealth you will create. I have hung out with people who start screaming and shouting at the littlest incident. It is no fun. It is not fun being in a car with someone who is driving and has road rage. They end up ruining the mood for everyone else in the car.

You need to let go of the outcome. So what if you lost some money. So what if you got laid off. You need to let go as the more wealth you create, the more responsibilities you will need to handle. Right now it could be you in your bedroom programming but at some other stage you could have a team of 10 employees. When I first became an entrepreneur, I thought I would have freedom, instead I found that I had a responsibility to my employees to do well in business otherwise they would lose their source of income.

This reminds me of a Chinese proverb:

Sāi Wēng lived on the border and he raised horses for a living. One day, he lost one of his prized horses.

After hearing of the misfortune, his neighbour felt sorry for him and came to comfort him. But Sāi Wēng simply asked, "How could we know it is not a good thing for me?"

After a while, the lost horse returned and with another beautiful horse. The neighbour came over again and congratulated Sāi Wēng on his good fortune. But Sāi Wēng simply asked, "How could we know it is not a bad thing for me?"

One day, his son went out for a ride with the new horse. He was violently thrown from the horse and broke his leg. The neighbours once again expressed their condolences to Sāi Wēng, but Sāi Wēng simply said, "How could we know it is not a good thing for me?".

One year later, the Emperor's army arrived at the village to recruit all able-bodied men to fight in the war. Because of his injury, Sāi Wēng's son could not go off to war, and was spared from certain death.

The more you can learn to deal with stress the further you will go. Remember that this earth is just a bunch of games created by humans. Even currency is a game. It is almost never as bad in retrospect as it seems and even if it is such bad news there is probably only a limited amount you can do about it. There are many resources online to help you deal with stress better. I have even taken coaching for anxiety when I was in the most uncertain stages of business with Scott Mooney (www.AnxietyGone.org). This helped me deal with it as having a coach helps.

You too can find books or other materials that will help you learn to cope with stress or anxiety better.

26.   You Have the Tools to Create Wealth

Figure 26-1: Sending a brick at a time is not as effective as it could be.

When walking past a building site in Islamabad, Pakistan I saw the above situation. It was basically a bricklayer on the ground floor throwing bricks up to his colleague on the first floor. I saw them doing this for a good 20 minutes before I moved on. Brick by brick.

Wealthology   AmirAnzur.com

In Europe or the US, the person would have probably had a tool like a forklift which would have moved all the bricks to the first floor within 15 minutes rather than 8 hours that it would have taken these two construction workers.

This was one of those lightbulb moments for me for one of the reasons why poverty happens. People simply have better tools in some parts of the world than they do in other parts of the world. Some people are looking to move from walking to a bicycle. Others are looking to upgrade their bicycle to a motorbike. While others are moving their motorbike to a car.

For producing physical goods, it may take countries like Pakistan a lot longer to catchup to countries like the US as they don't have the money to invest in tools like forklifts. But when it comes to the digital economy, the transition could be a lot faster. For instance, many of my team use laptops with 16 GB RAM. I am currently using a relatively top end laptop with 32 GB RAM. Although it is faster, for most tasks such as word processing or posting on social media you won't be able to notice the difference in the tool.

Now everyone is getting access to the same tools, and this is revolutionary. This is why I switched from iPhone to Android and from Mac to PC as I wanted to be on the same technology that most of the world could afford.

If I asked you to dig a deep hole, would you use a shovel or a teaspoon? Well, this depends, if you were getting paid hourly you might use a teaspoon. But most of us want to get done as much as quickly as possible as that is how entrepreneurs and wealth is created.

72

Figure 26-2: I use multiple screens as these tools allow me to produce more per hour of my time.

I have optimised my phone so that the right apps appear on my home screen in the right folders. I have optimised my home setup so that I have four computer screens while I do my work. These are the tools of the Internet economy, and you also need to optimize. This is what I teach in my courses, simply knowledge about the latest tools and techniques that I learn from around the world.

Sweden has one of the highest digital start-up rates per capita in the world. One of the reasons was that in the late 1990s the government sent laptops to every family so that everyone could get digital faster. You also need to petition your government to get a laptop in every home and to provide fast internet as soon as possible.

27.   Beards, Punks and Tattoos

Another pattern I have observed in rich people is they mostly conform to the normal. If you observe corporate people, who tend to be the highest paid, they don't have visible tattoos, funky hair or long beards. Of course, I am generalising as the outliers make a lot of wealth with this, but it all comes down to trust.

Whom would you trust more – a doctor with a large number of tattoos on their hands and face – or one that dresses well, is clean shaven and "looks the part" of a doctor?

This is up to you. You might feel that material wealth is not what you want to chase so you could sacrifice a bit of wealth and lose a few customers for the pleasure of being able to dress down or make your body appear the way you want.

Learn though that wealth is easier to create if you conform to what the society accepts as a trustable and hardworking person.

If you are preaching or for religious reasons you may want beards or other symbols of your faith but just know there will be a certain segment of the society that will discriminate because of that. It doesn't mean everyone. And it doesn't mean you should let this stop you as many are successful getting customers in their own reach, but I am talking about creating global brands. You might find that your niche likes your tattoos or religious symbols but in general to reach the masses it is more difficult.

The better dressed and corporate you can look, the more you are likely to earn. And unfortunately, that also means getting in shape – obese people also get discriminated against. I don't mean for this to hurt your self-esteem, but these are observations of many years of wealth creation – the more corporate, healthy and "normal" you look the easier to create wealth.

There are many studies that show better looking people can earn a better income but that might be a few percentage points and with all things being equal. If you outwork them, you can earn more.

The good news is that this will change in the digital economy, but it may take some time for people to truly stop discriminating. Everyone though can look at least a little better through better exercise, diet or clothing. I leave it to you to see how much you want it.

28. Pick Your Vehicle for Wealth Creation

There are an infinite number of ways to create wealth and I have categorised some of the major ones:

Career – This could be working as a teacher, doctor, lawyer or janitor. A career is what most people have and depending on the company you have joined there could be a lot of wealth that you can possibly create. Many careers can lead you to becoming a millionaire but chances of becoming a billionaire through a traditional career are minimal (and you by no means need to be a billionaire to be classified as wealthy!). The good thing is this is probably the safest route to go and if you are lucky enough to be in the right career for you can bring you passion and joy. The only downside might be your earning potential but for most people it meets their needs.

Property – You can invest in property alongside your career. This is how many people have a significant amount of their wealth invested in. They can leverage their money. For instance, paying 10 % deposit on a USD 1,000,000 home and if that home goes up just 10 % in value, they double their 10 % investment. Unless you are into renovations though there is little you can do to influence the price of the market as that is depended on the economy, neighbourhood and finding the right buyer. Investing in property can bring a lot of headaches too such as dealing with bad tenants but if you are willing to take the risk and learn to do it well there can be substantial financial reward.

Commodities – Gold, silver and even bitcoin I consider a commodity. You can buy them and hold on to them or trade them. You can make money as they go up or down. Bitcoin can fluctuate a lot more but in essence it is like a commodity like gold and silver that you cannot control the price of (unless you are a huge player like Elon Musk who can fluctuate the price to a certain extent).

Shares – Shares, bonds etc are also traded in the market and if you have a good eye for them, you can make money trading. Investors like Warren Buffet can outperform the market as they research the market and can have an educated guess of which companies are undervalued. You can be an investor into businesses such as start-ups. This means you risk your capital but someone else does the work. For instance, when Jeff Bezos started Amazon in 1994, he got 20 investors to invest USD 50,000 each. If those investors had held on to their shares, they would have been worth over USD 50,000,000 by 2021.

Traditional Businesses – You can invest in a restaurant such as a McDonalds franchise or setup another physical business. These can cost you anything from a few thousand dollars to a few million dollars to setup. As a business owner you do have the chance of getting rich but do expect to work long hours in the early days especially and your capital is again at risk.

Digital Products – You can also make money through digital businesses. This can include selling digital courses or services or software. You can get started on these for as little as no investment, but they usually still take time. This is what my team also helps deliver through aartec. Experience leads you to make digital products cheaper and cheaper. YouTube videos, friends on facebook, Twitter followers are all examples of digital assets. Non-Fungible Tokens, Software As A Service (SAAS) and other virtual products will only grow over the next decade.

Inherit Wealth – At least 20 % of people simply get wealthy by inheriting their wealth. You might not have much choice in this except being good to your parents if they are rich!

Marry Well – You could also pick a partner who is wealthy and there is nothing wrong with being a "gold digger", it is another path to success. My hypothesis is that richer people are more likely to divorce as money gives them the option of not having to stay in an unhappy marriage as they can both afford to leave and look after themselves if things don't work out.

You need to pick your own vehicle for wealth creation. For instance, I have property, stocks and even cryptocurrency but all this is just dabbling. My real vehicles for wealth creation is my online businesses such as AmirAnzur.com (coaching and consulting) as well as aartec.com (delivering digital innovations) as well as other digital products and services.

29.   There Are More Rich People Than You Think

There are 350,000 millionaires in London (population 9 million). One in 26 people in London is a dollar millionaire.

There are 18.6 million millionaires in the US (population 330 million). One in 18 people in the US is a dollar millionaire.

I wanted to help the poorest of society, but I learned that I made the most money from helping the richest of society. They tend to spend the most on their personal development and have the most money to invest in new ventures and try new ideas.

If you target the richest of society you have an easier chance of creating wealth than targeting the poorest of society. Seems obvious, but it took me a while to figure this out. The reason that American companies can become richer quicker than Pakistani companies is that their populations have more money to spend so they have more customers quicker than Pakistani innovators who have less people able to spend money with them.

For instance, when I first started coaching and consulting in 2010, I was able to charge a rich European student USD 30,000 for how to launch their business online. When I moved to Pakistan and started charging USD 100, I still struggled and could only attract the very elite of society with that price.

This changes in the Internet economy though where you can target customers from anywhere. The world becomes more competitive.

If you stop being a mappest and only thinking about your community you will be poorer than when you start thinking of humanity as a whole.

What can you target that will fulfil the needs of the rich rather than the poor of society? Once you can make your money, you can always help the poorest.

For me creating personal wealth wasn't always the highest priority target. What I have learnt over my journey is that not everyone is driven to just help the rich or chase money.

Some people just want to be great teachers, or doctors, or pilots – wealth is not at the top of their agenda. That is fine as not everyone is cut out for and wants to generate a bigger number on a database to stroke their ego on how much wealth they have created. We need both parts of society in order to have a healthy society.

Offshoring or outsourcing doesn't mean that the rich countries will lose all their employment. But it simply means that they will focus on creating substantial wealth and the lower value work can be done cheaper somewhere else. This was exactly how Nike worked over the past few decades having high value people like Michael Jordan create the brand in the US while low value production was done in Vietnam and China. Most of the iPhone is also built-in factories in China but there is substantial high end work done in the United States.

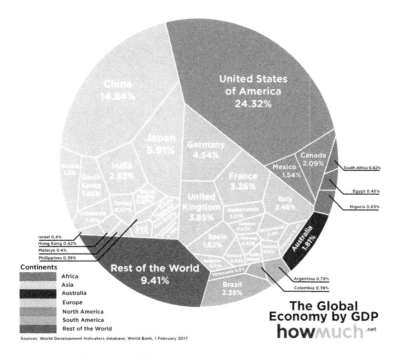

Figure 29-1: One in four dollars spent around the world is done so in the US.

In the above chart you see that 24.32 % of the world economy is the United States. This means that almost one out of every four dollars spent around the world was done in the United States.

The United Kingdom has the highest spend online per capita at GBP 3,041 (USD 4,200) beating even their richer American counterparts.

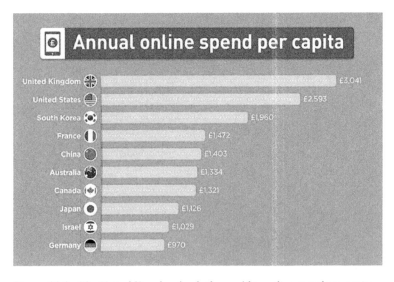

Figure 29-2 - The United Kingdom leads the world in online spend per capita.
Source: Insightdiy.co.uk

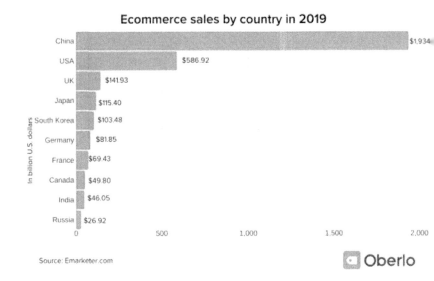

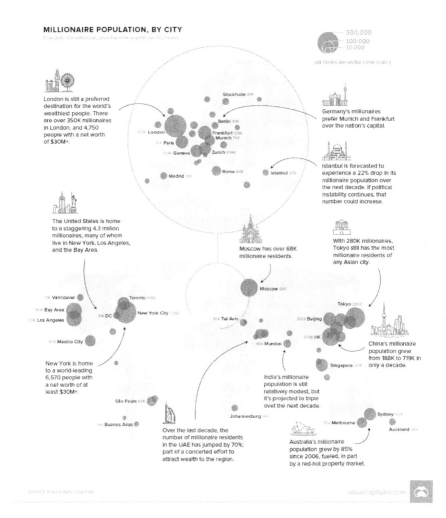

MILLIONAIRE POPULATION, BY CITY

China might have the highest sales of ecommerce in the world, but it is probably easier for you to market to the American market as they understand the English language and you probably know more about American culture through Hollywood than Chinese culture.

There are rich people everywhere, but they are at a greater density in places like New York, London, Hong Kong or Tokyo.

83

The good news is that the number of people living in
extreme poverty around the world is also decreasing at a
substantial rate.

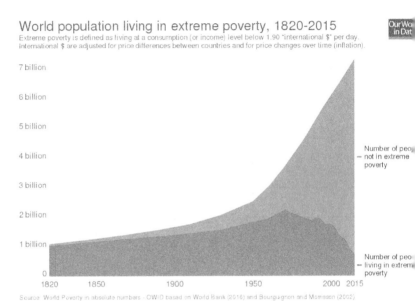

World population living in extreme poverty, 1820-2015

Extreme poverty is defined as living at a consumption (or income) level below 1.90 "international $" per day.
International $ are adjusted for price differences between countries and for price changes over time (inflation).

Source: World Poverty in absolute numbers - OWID based on World Bank (2016) and Bourguignon and Morrison (2002)

30.   Beware of Survivorship Bias

One of the things that I have learned in the online world is the survivorship bias. This is the ad you see where someone is pitching their product or service such as making money through Amazon, Instagram or Facebook marketing.

What I have learned though is that everyone is unique, and everyone has their own path to creating wealth. You cannot expect to copy Warren Buffet's strategy and make money in the same way – he had access to contacts, knowledge and experience that you might not have access to.

Not everyone can post on social media and grow a following – you simply might not be as interesting as Kim Kardashian or have the physical appearance of Kendal Jenner to make millions online. Your culture might not also allow you to do the risky things that others in an American culture might be able to do for example.

I see online gurus all the time convincing their followers to follow a certain path to wealth creation. And I see most of their followers failing in that path. If there was a guaranteed and easy path to wealth creation than it wouldn't be as lucrative as everyone would be doing it.

Don't even listen to me when it comes to wealth creation. In this book, I outline some wealth creation strategies, but they might not necessarily work for you. My intention is at least to get you thinking about the path to wealth creation, the actual journey will be different for each one of you.

Remember that your own journey will be unique. You can follow many gurus and you can take many courses but ultimately you will define your own path.

31.   There is Too Much Choice

The good news today is that you probably have all the money you need, you simply have to focus on less not more. Walk into a decent grocery store and you will see dozens of types of drinks that you can drink and dozens of types of cereals you can eat. Ask most nutritionists though it would be best for you to go to the vegetable isle and only shop there and only drink the plain water.

You will not only save yourself a ton of money but also get yourself into the best shape. The trick is to avoid 98 % of the food available in a grocery store and pick from the 2 % which is actually healthy for you.

If you go eat at the Michelin star or at high end places where rich people tend to eat you will notice that the quantity of food is less than where poorer people tend to eat. You need less sugary drinks. Less junk food. Less of most things you see in the grocery store.

You don't need a big house that can clutter up your life. Learn to live simply. Eat. Drink. Consume. Less. Not more.

Remember long term you will feel better having the right amount of weight on your body than you will having a big amount of money in your bank account. Getting in shape is something you can work on without much investment and can have a better return on your happiness than a flashy new car or bigger house.

In the UK, I have been in the top 1 % of earners (to be in the top 1 % you need to earn over GBP 160,000 per year of taxable income) as well as been in the bottom 1 % of

earners – in the UK this meant that I collected benefits
from the government as my business had not worked out
and I was unemployed. Yes, life was different. But much
of it was psychological. When I was collecting
unemployment benefits my self-esteem was down. I was
also taking money from my parents at the same time.

The thing we have to help people who do go unemployed
or homeless is with their self-esteem and self-worth. You
do not need to tie it in with what you are earning. The
number in your bank account is not equal to what you are
worth to the world.

Figure 31-1: Sometimes less is more. The healthiest drink is plain old water.

32.   The Money is in the Brand

Michael Jordan made USD 130 million from Nike in 2019 – 16 years since he last played professional basketball. Tiger Woods has grossed over USD 1 billion in his career primarily from sponsorships.

The shoes that Michael Jordan sold – the Nike Air Jordan – were manufactured in countries like Vietnam. Making shoes was the low value work. The higher value work was creating the brand so that people desired to "be like Mike". You too will have to think long term about brands and how to create them. The good thing is that you don't need an MBA to learn about brand creation. You can learn about it by following actual brands and what they do. You can copy their strategies.

Just remember though those brands can take a significant amount of money to build but you just need to be aware that brands exist, and long-term wealth creation is through brand building. A brand is basically a promise.

McDonalds promises you that you will get a certain quality of burger in a short amount of time. Boeing promises you a safe flight. FedEx promises you that your parcels will get to their recipients in a short amount of time. Louis Vuitton promises you quality handbags.

Nike promises you quality shoes and the chance to be associated with the best athletes in the world. What will your brand promise?

Figure 32-1: Michael Jordan holding a Nike Air Jordan shoe.

Figure 32-2: A Made in Vietnam label inside a Nike shoe.

Figure 32-3: Tiger Woods could always be seen wearing the Nike logo when he had the sponsorship.

33. Learn the Laws of Luxury

As should be obvious, the rich have more money to spend. They are also more likely to spend that money. What can you do to create a luxury brand? How can your clients feel special?

You can learn the laws of luxury in whatever segment you are in. The challenge with going for the cheapest is that someone can always come in cheaper than you. How can you raise your quality and go for luxury?

When you go for luxury, you need to get less clients and can give them each more time. Let's say that a typical property dealer makes 1 % of the property they sell. Will they make more selling more expensive homes or cheaper homes?

How can you raise your standards so that you aim at a higher earning segment of society?

One of the best lessons I learned from my USD 100,000 MBA at IMD Business School, Switzerland was when the 90 of us students were divided into groups of 10 and told to create a handbag and sell it. We were given certain materials and told to price it and depending on the material we would know our profit margins.

Most of our groups were trying to price it between USD 60 and USD 100. The group that won the competition priced their bag at USD 12,000. They managed to sell three of those pretend bags (we were a rich Swiss school!). They brought in a VIP club with the bag and other luxuries. They only had to sell one bag and made more than all the other teams combined.

Scarcity brings in luxury. For instance, the Swiss will launch only a certain number of Patek Phillippe watches, or the French will only have a certain number of wines from 1977 or Ferrari will only have a certain number of cars released each year – not because demand isn't there, but because they have demand precisely because they have so few in production.

This is how Americans have also created wealth. As an example, you can buy baseball cards which are limited to 1,000 cards to be released of Michael Jordan's rookie season. Then kids and adults will trade these cards for other cards or money. This is how Non-fungible Tokens have come about with people paying for the privilege of saying they own a rare piece of digital art.

You should also look at what you can do to enter the luxury economy.

35.   Money Makes Money

It is a lot easier to make money when you have money. Of course, when you don't have money, you can't hire employees or spend on online software or hire an accountant or invest in a business or property.

But you can start with no money and still get there - it just might take you a little longer and you might have to get a bit more creative. You can get a loan from a friend, family or bank. You can get an investor onboard.   You can give away shares of your business to co-founders you can't afford to hire. If you have a great opportunity that you are passionate about you can make it happen. Be creative.

It is not necessarily a bad thing to have loans or be in debt. Even Apple which is worth over a trillion dollars has some debt. Entrepreneurs like Donald Trump borrowed money to make their construction projects happen. Almost every billionaire has had to learn to deal with debt or selling equity in their business. They haven't done it by starting out with a bunch of cash.

Of course, it is easier if you are born rich because even if you don't have the money yourself, you are more likely to have a network of people that have access to capital and might be willing to invest in you or loan you the money.

Most great entrepreneurs will keep reinvesting the money they make into other businesses and ventures. They don't just let the cash pile in the bank. Cash sitting around isn't as useful as being used to fund some venture or project.

People with a lot of cash are looking for entrepreneurs like you so that they can get a better return on their investment than what the bank gives them. There are different challenges to having a lot of wealth than having no wealth, but they are still challenges.

I remember telling a friend how lucky he was to be inheriting a business that was doing several hundred million dollars a year. He told me "but my father has built it up over his lifetime and what if I screw it up and all the employees lose their jobs?" Your money problems won't go away once you make x amount of money. There will just be different challenges.

There is no "someday when I make x amount there will be a happily ever after". Your journey keeps continuing even when you reach the happily ever after. You will still get sick - which can be more stressful than money. You will still eat roughly the same.

Money makes money but it doesn't have to be your money which makes the money. A bank could loan you the money at 5 % interest rate and if you are able to make money at a 10 % return you can do well. This is how a lot of wealth is created in the developed world.

Take the concept of mortgages. This is basically where the bank helps you buy a house you could not afford by yourself. A house might be worth USD 1,000,000 and you only have USD 100,000. The bank agrees to loan you the USD 900,000 if you put in 10 % (or USD 100,000).

They will charge you a 5 % interest rate per year which roughly equals USD 900,000 * .05 = USD 45,000. Lets say that in 10 years the value of your property doubles to USD 2,000,000. Then from your USD 100,000 you have made USD 1,000,000 profit minus the USD 45,000 * 10 years of interest or roughly your USD 100,000 has turned into USD 500,000 with the banks help.

This is how so much of the wealth is generated in the developed world. If you go to a country like Pakistan very few people are getting mortgages as banks only offer them to very few people and at 18 % interest rate which doesn't make it worth their while.

In the same regard you could ask an investor to invest in your startup app business and if they invest USD 100,000, they get 10 % of your business. This would value your business at USD 1,000,000 and technically already raise your net worth to USD 900,000 overnight. If you create the next Facebook their USD 100,000 could be worth over a billion dollars.

When you start to understand the world of finance your brain starts really to understand how true wealth is created. This is why some of the richest cities are places like New York, London and Hong Kong. There is so much access to capital there that people can go do many ideas - from constructing buildings to starting banks.

It used to be that to get access to this capital you needed to be near the banks. Now though you can do it online from almost anywhere but I do think even in 2022 it helps to be able to meet people and bankers face to face.

Some of my students who have had no money to start their business have borrowed upto USD 35,000 from sites like StartupLoans.co.uk. The British government backs the loans so that it makes it easier for entrepreneurs to start their ventures.

Or a great scheme in the UK is the Seed Enterprise Investment Scheme where if a UK tax payer invests in a startup, the government gives 50 % of their investment back to them. And if the startup was to fail within three years, the government would give a further 25 % back to them so the most they could lose is 25 % of their investment. And if the company was to make money, they don't have to pay any capital gains tax on it.

Most governments around the world want to encourage entrepreneurship as entrepreneurs create employment and once they are successful pay taxes too. So look out for grants and incentives in your country that make it easier to get money to help you make more money.

36.   Talk To Strangers

Some of the wealthiest people I have met are in their core salespeople. They need to convince customers to buy their products or services. They need to convince employees to join their company. They need to convince suppliers to work with them.

One thing I learned from great salespeople is that they talk to everyone. Despite the advice we got at a young age of not talking to strangers, they talk to people. These talks lead to opportunities or simply an exchange of knowledge.

You have probably heard the expression that "your network is your net worth" and I completely agree with this. There are many people I know who even if they lost all their wealth would regain it very quickly simply because of who they know and how they are able to negotiate deals with them.

The more you talk to people, the better you will get at talking to people. Make small talk. I compliment the cashier at the supermarket about her tattoo. Or ask my barber where he comes from originally. Or ask the concierge at the hotel I am staying at what are the best places to visit. Or ask the waiter who is serving me what dishes he recommends or how long he has worked there.

It doesn't matter what the initial question is. Ask how they are doing. Make a small comment. It leads to other comments and a conversation. A good conversation will boost your self-esteem. It will teach you that we have more in common with people than we think. Or that many people have different viewpoints to us but that is OK.

Learn to make friends. This means caring about people. Not always thinking about what you can get from them, but to really think about how you can help them.

When I used to try to make a sale, I would be focused on how much I could charge the client. Money was top of my mind (when you are a hungry entrepreneur it is difficult to not think of the money!). Now, I think if and how I can help them. If I don't think I can, then I don't push for the sale. If I think I can then I present them a solution to their problem. If they are interested only then I start thinking about price and the formalities. Money is simply an exchange of energy. It becomes more a formality.

Prospecting is what will help you get more sales. Especially if you are starting a business, look at your empty calendar and look to fill it up. I contact old school friends, university friends, work colleagues and even strangers on LinkedIn to see if they want to have a virtual or physical coffee. I meet them to find out more about them and what they are doing and what their interests are. This is all for free and might even cost me the price of the lunch. But some of these meeting lead to business opportunities. I have so many different businesses and ways to deliver that I can refer them to someone or build technology for them or offer another solution. Or simply help them brainstorm a solution for their own life. If they like the way you think they will refer people to you.

You are building a brand, one stranger at a time. All these little interactions will help not only build your confidence but your wealth. Know the people in your community. Look up your neighbors. Speak to your professors outside class. Speak to the janitor. These strangers will give you different perspectives on life.

Everyone is important. The janitor or secretary have their own network which could potentially help you even if they can't help you themselves.

Of course, some people are more important than others. I call these kingpins. The kingpin is the pin in bowling that is in front which bowls over all the other pins. These will be the people with strong networks - you contact Tony and Tony knows people that can help you raise the money or find the employees or make an introduction to a journalist. These kingpins have their relationships as their assets.

Figure 36-1: The kingpin is the pin in front which knocks out all the other pins

37.   Relationships Are Your Third Biggest Asset

Relationships are an asset. People will buy from people that they know, like and trust. In this regard social media has enabled people to scale up their relationships – they get to know more people.

How can you build more relationships? I take the time out to write hand-written cards to friends, clients and even employees at occasions like New Years. Could you also do that to your clients? Relationships can take years to build.

Having worked with some of the largest companies and having sold millions of dollars of products and services, I can state that it comes down to clients knowing you, liking you and trusting you.

Don't only focus on clients as your relationships. Your employees and suppliers also need to love working with you and they can have a bigger impact than some of your clients.

I ask to connect to people on Facebook, LinkedIn, Twitter, Instagram and whatever social media I can. Your address book is your asset. When I enter a phone number in my mobile, I use keywords like "John Smith London JP Morgan IMD Business School Barbara 2021". This may mean that a few months or years down the line I might not remember the name John Smith but I might then search "IMD" or "London" to see if I can shortlist the names. I might also search by "Barbara" as I know that I know John through Barbara.

I might even put in the notes field that John has two sons aged 10 and 13 and lives in Clapham.

How can you build and scale your relationships as you go through your career?

38.   Know the Traditional Ways of Making Money – but don't get FOMO

Everyone will be talking about property or bitcoin or some other way of making money. Don't get Fear of Missing Out (FOMO). Plan a strategy for yourself and stick to it as long as you can. Almost anybody can make money in a chosen wealth creation platform – whether it be property, software development or trading.

You will just need to work hard and smart in order to get there and don't get distracted by the dozens of opportunities that will present themselves as you fear that you will miss out. Salespeople exist everywhere including behind some of the stories you read in the newspapers trying to get you to buy into their opportunity.

As I type this there is a lot of hype about bitcoin. I could abandon my own goals and start searching on it but instead I have chosen to focus on how I think I can improve the world rather than what others want me to look at.

Buying property was another thing I learned is not necessarily for everyone. You could use that cash to invest in your business instead of being tied down with a mortgage. Pick your vehicle for wealth creation and focus on that. Looking at houses isn't what gives me pleasure – building businesses and writing books does. You do you. I do me.

39. My Wealthy Appy Life

You don't need much income to live a relatively happy and wealthy life. For instance, this is how I live even though I might be in the higher income bracket. You can do the same without much deviation.

I have a Spotify subscription for USD 10 per month. This gives me access to pretty much all songs I can ever think of. When I am feeling in a bad mood or just feel like dancing I search for a song on Spotify and it immediately puts me in a better mood. Access to this amazing music library for just USD 10 per month. Recently, Spotify started putting lyrics to songs too so you can sing along.

If I am ever at a restaurant and hear a song that I like but don't know what it is, I use Shazam which has this incredible algorithm to listen to the song, search the millions of songs available and then tell me the name of the song and the artist. All for free. I then listen to that song some other time on Spotify and add it to my playlists. I can go for a walk in the park (for free) and sing along to my favorite songs all for free.

When I was a kid growing up in the 1980s and 1990s I would have had to go to a record store and pay USD 15 for an album which had 10 songs on it with only one or two that I actually liked. Maybe if you are under 20 years old, you don't appreciate it but as I am over 40 I appreciate this aspect of my life - especially if I am ever feeling down.

For food I use an app called Gorillas.io which allows me to order most items from a standard supermarket and for USD 3 for the delivery charge. They deliver it to me within 10 minutes of me placing the order. I try to eat vegetables and simple food which is not only cheaper than processed food but is a lot healthier for you. Occasionally if I need fancier food or have a dinner party at home I use an app like Uber Eats or Deliveroo to deliver me the food for the guests without having to cook it from hundreds of restaurants.

If I need a cleaner to clean up after me at the dinner party and don't have my regular cleaner available, I can use the Handy app to order me the cleaner within a few hours.

If I go on a juice cleanse diet, I use Fuel-station.co.uk which sends me the fresh juices for my 10-day juice fasts. For regular meals I use KeyToFood.co.uk which delivers me the next days meals (I can choose the exact number of calories I want and the types of food). These are super easy to heat up and eat. I essentially don't have to think about my food, which saves me time to think about my work such as writing this book.

If people want to schedule an appointment with me I ask them to visit www.calendly.com/amiranzur as it saves me from hiring a secretary and the back and forth emails as this has my calendar integrated and they can pick a time slot themselves to book the call. This is a free app but I pay the USD 10 per month for the premium features. If you want to book a call with me you can use the calenly link provided above.

I use the weather app on my phone to make the unpredictable British weather more predictable for me. It tells me for the day what each hour is going to look like and the chances of rain in any given hour. It tells me the forecast for the 10 days ahead too. This is all free.

If I need to book an appointment with my doctor, I can use the NHS app to do so. Previously this would involve me having to call and wait on the phone to speak to a human which wasted my time. My doctors' appointments are now usually on the phone too whereas pre-corona I would have had to take time off work to visit the clinic which would have taken more time out of my day.

I have my medicine prescribed online and I use Well.co.uk app to order the medicine so it is delivered to my home within a few days and I don't need to visit the pharmacy. My doctors clinic directly communicates with my pharmacy to approve the prescription. I can order any medicine directly from the NHS app and without having to speak to a human, it gets delivered to my home for free.

If I need to brush up on my French and learn Spanish I use the DuoLingo App while waiting somewhere.

I don't own a car as I live in London and the public transport is so good. This means that when I am travelling I am actually using my time productively. While I am walking or travelling on the bus or tube I listen to audiobooks on Audible where some of the greatest authors (including me!) have their books in an audio version so that even while I am walking or travelling, I am learning. This costs me roughly USD 10 per book but is well worth the investment. Audiobooks are even better than podcasts as the authors usually put more thought into their content and revise it a few times. Even if you are catching only 70 % of the content as you are focusing else where it is still good – most authors repeat the same points multiple times anyway. I listen to the audiobooks at 1.5 times normal speed, so I get through them quicker.

When I can't use public transport, I use companies like Uber which offer me a private chauffer to pick me from exactly where I am to where I want to go, without worrying about parking or having cash or taking out my credit card as it is set in the app. This is also much cheaper than the black cabs that existed in London and were limited in supply.

When I need to travel by public transport I use CityMapper App as it even tells me if I am using a train whether to sit in the front of the train carriage as that is where the exit to the station where I am heading is or at the back of the train as my next connecting train or exit will be towards the rear of the train. It will tell me exactly how many minutes till the next bus arrives and when I am on the bus it will even buzz me telling me that it is time to get off so I don't miss my bus stop. All this for free.

When I need to get my own car as the public transport or Uber are not sufficient to get away for the weekend, I can use an app like GetAround where people rent out their cars like AirBnB does with people's spare rooms. Instead of going to car rental places like Avis and Hertz which were usually located near airports or main railway stations, I can collect my rental GetAround car from somewhere near my neighborhood. ZipCar offers a similar service but you can rent by the hour.

I have all my banking apps on my phone so I can always check how much money I have and if I need to pay someone I can do so straight from my phone. I also have my accounting software, xero, on my phone so I can check the status of my companies at any moment. All these apps are organized in a special "finance" folder on my phone so that I can find them easily on my phone. If I need to pay someone instantly I can use Remitly or Wise to transfer money around the world much cheaper than the traditional banking apps.

In the "social media" folder, I can check-in with how my friends are doing. I can keep prospecting for sales by reaching out to prospects on apps like LinkedIn or Facebook while on the bus so I don't waste time. When I started my career in the 1990s pre-internet the best I could do was to buy a magazine at a train station to keep me occupied - now my travel time is actually used to generate wealth as I know the more people I can speak to or meet, the more wealth I am likely to generate.

While I am travelling and I have an idea for a book or a website I use the EverNote app to write it down so I have thousands of thoughts and ideas on it which I can access when I am travelling or at home. It even syncs with my computer so that I can transfer thoughts from my phone to my laptop like I have done just now. I pay for the premium version which is USD 40 per year. I also use the OneNote app which has similar features to EverNote.

I have my Google calendar on my phone so I always know when I have a meeting and where I need to be. I send meeting invites to people's email addresses so they are booked in both our diaries.

Google calendar connects to Google Maps so that it can guide me to where I need to walk to. Google Maps allows me to navigate almost any city in the world without being lost. My email is also on my phone so that I can answer emails while travelling.

I can also use Keep Notes app which has my daily, weekly, monthly, yearly and lifetime goals list which I can remind myself of what I need to get done. Most successful people simply have set themselves better goals than less "successful" people.

I can shop on Amazon through their app and get millions of products delivered to my home the next day. Having access to reading a review is much more efficient way to be sold to than having a pushy salesman telling me what to buy in a real world retail store. Also it saves me from carrying the items home as a mailperson will do it for me. The "Amazon's Choice" tag also saves me time as this is the item they recommend taking the price, returns and reviews in consideration.

I have YouTube on my phone to go through other content if I don't feel like listening to my Audible. I also have thousands of movies available on my phone through the NetFlix and Amazon Prime Video Apps to keep me entertained at about USD 10 per month.

If you want to find someone romantically you don't have to go to a bar like you did in my day and be an extrovert to chat up people. You can use Tinder or Bumble or go into niche sites like Jdate (for Jews looking for dates) or Muzz (for Muslims looking to date other Muslims).

I sometimes use the Strava App when I am exercising so it tracks my jogs to see how consistently I am exercising and how far I have run and in how much time.

I use the LaundryHeap app which sends someone to collect my laundry and deliver it 24 hours later back to be washed and ironed.

If I ever have a problem with my laptop, Nerdapp.com will send an IT support engineer to my home for USD 80 per hour or USD 20 remotely.

Of course I also have the camera on my phone so I can take pictures of my son anytime I see a moment worth capturing.

I use the alarm app to set multiple alarms throughout the day so set and forget. For instance if I have to board a flight in 30 minutes I set it on my phone so that I can do other things and forget about it - setting multiple alarms throughout the day such as for meetings, flights and calls is a great way to go about your day and focus on the task at hand without worrying about missing anything.

I also have my authenticator app on my phone which allows me to more securely login to websites such as Stripe and Facebook to keep things more secure.

I have the SquareUp app so that I can sell my books to people and take their credit cards when I am physically with them. I can check my Stripe account to see how my sales are doing online.

I use WhatsApp Business version app to be able to make calls around the world for free as well as track incoming enquiries (WhatsApp Business is another version of WhatsApp which is useful for running small businesses as it allows you to track leads and sell products). You can WhatsApp me on +447733003930.

I use the voice recorder if I ever want to record a voice note for myself or record a podcast. I can use Facebook to broadcast a live interview. I can hookup my external microphone to my phone and get interviews with people. This would have cost thousands of dollars just a few decades ago.

All these apps cost less than USD 50 per month for me to live this extraordinary and amazing life. This is truly amazing and if you are in your 40s or older like I am you appreciate it even more as you see how far human society has developed in the past two decades alone.

If I ever feel down I remind myself of this fact. When I take on coaching clients I teach them how to optimize their phones and their laptops so their life is optimized. Even if they are super high net worth clients they end up feeling that for less than USD 50 a month they drastically change the quality of their life. You don't need coaching from me. Simply use the above or speak to friends and ask them what apps and websites they use or research them online. You will be amazed.

These apps have taken millions of dollars to build and a billionaire has access to the same apps as you do for the same price. But just like knowledge, apps are not as useful unless they are applied.

Figure 39-1- You can use your apps anywhere

40.   Be Hungry

The amount of wealth you can create in your life is up to you. Work longer hours, you will likely create more wealth. Learn more and you will likely create more wealth. Connect to wealthier people and you will likely create more wealth.

The bigger the goals you have, the more you will persevere through the hard times. Be hungry.

One of the things I noticed with some of my richer friends that inherited wealth is that they were not necessarily hungry for wealth creation. They didn't have the passion to help the world in any way. They were satisfied to live their life.

There isn't anything wrong with that, but I think if you can give yourself more motivation you work harder. For me although my corporate paths would make me a millionaire almost guaranteed – if I had the patience – I felt that there was more I needed to do to help end poverty.

This drives me. Although it means sacrifice of time and income in the short term, in the long term you get the rewards. Think of something bigger than yourself and it will make you hungry to go out and chase that dream.

Yes, this may mean sacrifice of family time. Read up about Bill Gates, Warren Buffett, Elon Musk or Jeff Bezos who have all gotten divorces as their partners complain of how much time they commit to their businesses. You don't need to be single, but I am pointing out that creating wealth does take time, energy and experimentation.

Bill, Warren, Elon and Jeff could have retired a long time ago but they choose to create wealth so they can help more people. Remember that wealth creation is a game, and the purpose of the game is to help as many people as possible.

41.   Be Aware of Time Sucks

Just as when you walk into a grocery store and get distracted by all the items you could buy rather than what you should buy, there are time sucks in your life which take your focus away from what you should be doing.

You need to focus on creating an amazing product or service – the rest is secondary. You need to spend less time on Facebook/Instagram/YouTube and focus on your craft. Yes, you need to spend time on educating yourself but be aware of over-educating yourself at the risk of action.

I have a minimal number of apps on my phone especially on my home screen. Almost all are business related such as banking apps. If I do check social media, it is to study how to market using it. I save the ads that are marketing to me so I can take ideas from them. But I have to be extremely careful not to get sucked into endless people stalking. You too need to figure out how to focus in order to get to your goals faster.

Have uninterrupted focussed time. You can even set the timer on your phone to give you 55 minutes of uninterrupted time to focus on your craft.

You can put your phone on airplane mode and focus – you won't miss anything. In this information economy, your ability to focus is a true asset.

Your ability to focus is like a muscle which you can build over time.

One other tip for time saving is to outsource everything that is cheaper for someone else to do. For me for instance, I hired a voiceover talent to record my audiobook. I have a product manager that I feed my Internet ideas who turns them into reality and figures out the details.

You can hire people in a different part of the world as long as you give them the vision they will figure out the details. Remember that when you start to enter a project, the details always take time. For me, I have learned that I need to focus on the vision and creating content such as this book but not on the details of testing my software products or on invoicing customers or on customer support.

You need to focus on your highest value activities and outsource the rest.

42. Understand Affiliate Marketing

Another vehicle to wealth creation is affiliate marketing. This is where companies pay you to market their products and services for them.

For instance, a company is selling a course for USD 1,000. They can afford to give you USD 900 as a commission and still make USD 100 as profit. Many companies are giving large commissions for affiliates.

This means that you do not need to have your own products and services or handle customer service etc. You simply need to learn how to market. Companies like ClickBank.com and CJ.com have paid out over four billion dollars to affiliates.

You need to learn the skills of copywriting, social media marketing (paid ads not necessarily organic ads) so that you can market. If you can't find your own products and services to sell, you can sell other people's.

There is a variety of ways this can work. You can get a unique link like www.amiranzur.com/1 which would then tell the receiving site that you referred them. You can also get a unique coupon code like "AmirAnzur123" and that can give the buyer a USD 100 off and give you USD 100 commission.

Affiliate marketing will only grow in the Internet economy so you can learn this as a possible avenue for wealth creation. At the end of the day everyone makes a living from selling something and if you can learn to sell online, you can create a lot of wealth for yourself.

You can become an affiliate at AmirAnzur.com to see how you can help us market while making an income for yourself. If you let me know that you are referring a customer to me, I can even pay you an affiliate commission.

43.   The World Is Turning Less Corporate

In the last century the world had become very corporate. If you got a job in a respectable consulting company like Deloitte, KPMG, McKinsey or got into banking you could become a millionaire. These companies though expected you to look and act a certain way.

You needed certain dress code – big beards, face tattoos and long hair were not appropriate for instance and even if it wasn't written in the rule book, they were unwritten rules.

Now though I see more and more people in cities like London with their tattoos and beards. The old school me would have said, avoid them unless you are in the celebrity business like David Beckham. I would still agree to a certain degree that being clean shaven, dressing well etc will lead you to more wealth as more of the old school people are used to trusting people who conform to "normal" – but now the world is becoming less corporate.

It might take you a little longer to trust the opinion of a doctor who has tattoos all over his hands or face but more people are having this individuality and so more people are getting accustomed to it.

But again this is another thing for wealth creation you might not want to sacrifice. You might think that your need to dress a certain way or have certain hair or have certain tattoos are more important to you than to generate cash in your bank account.

Look for success models in your industry and follow them.

44. Become a Professional

You might see people sitting on the beach making money in Internet ads telling you how to make money online. In my experience, if you want to maximize your wealth you will have to become a professional. For most people this means having a home office or a proper office setup from where you can work regularly.

Cafés probably are not as efficient as a home office. As for your team if you can get them to work from an office, that is likely more efficient than working remotely. I am still old school about working from an office for most people especially the young as learning is accelerated and ideas flow better when people meet face to face rather than on Zoom meetings.

For myself and my Chief Technology Officer though we work remotely from our home offices. Both of us need focused time and if we are in an office environment we get disturbed too often with questions and firefighting problems.

I have three screen monitors setup so that I can do things like write my book in one monitor, keep a calendar open in another monitor and use the third to do any ad hoc research that might be needed as I write my book. You can't do this while working from a café. You will also notice a ring light behind my screen as well as an external camera so that I get better lighting on zoom calls and better quality images for my calls. You might also consider an external mic for better sound.

You need a setup that works for you. I do occasionally work from cafés but I am in my element when I am alone at home and working undisturbed. I think of myself as a professional. What is the most I can produce by the hour. What task out of all the tasks that I have pending will produce the best outcome for my team and I.

I pretty much sit in a windowless room and could be anywhere in the world. I also chose to settle in London as it gives me the best chance of wealth creation as I can meet people when required and it is one of the central hubs of the world. I don't suggest changing cities for the sake of it, but do you have a good network where you are? Cities like New York, London, San Francisco, Hong Kong are more likely to bring you wealth then smaller villages even as the world turns more remote. A face-to-face meeting will always bring more trust than a zoom meeting.

Am I more likely to bump into an executive from Google in London or on a beach in Bali? Serendipity, or as the dictionary defines it: the occurrence and development of events by chance in a happy or beneficial way, can happen anywhere but the chances increase in some cities and offices. This is why good schools or universities also allow for better serendipity as the chances of you running into more successful and richer people increase.

Thats why countries even build clusters of companies. For instance, in London we have Canary Wharf for banking, Silicon Roundabout for technology, Fleet Street for newspapers, Saville Row for tailoring and Harley Street for medical.

In Dubai, we have DIFC for finance, Academic City for universities, Internet City for technology startups etc. Embrace serendipity!

I read somewhere that if Nike had their offices in New York City instead of Beaverton, Oregon they would add a few billion dollars to their market capitalization. But the founder, Phil Knight, still chose Oregon. For various lifestyle and family purposes you might choose to live and work the way you do and ultimately wealth is about being happy than just chasing a number in a database.

I even have to stop myself from listening to music while I am working really focused so that I can produce output like a professional. The amateurs will want to create wealth but they want to show the world that they are sitting at the beach and partying while making money, the professionals are more than likely working long hours and perfecting their craft.

Just think to yourself - even if you are not making money yet -would a professional work the way I do?

45.   Mental Wealth

Wealth is created through creating value for the world but if you think about it all of wealth creation is simply a game. If you are a lawyer and you charge more hours to your clients, you will create more wealth.

If you are an entrepreneur and you sell more widgets, you will create more wealth. If you are an employee and you deliver to your bosses' expectations, you will create more wealth.

The challenge is that we should not just think of wealth as a number in a database but also mental wealth as well. Ultimately, saying that you are a billionaire, millionaire or financially independent is just a state of mind.

Financial wealth can impact our mental wealth considerably. You are stressed as you don't know if you will be able to pay your rent or your salaries. You are stressed as you would like to buy a better car or house.

But sometimes I look at the squirrel outside the window. If they don't gather any nuts that day, they could die. I have – out of choice rather than necessity – been able to live without food and drink only water for 10 days. There are people that have done over a month without food. This shows me that we can get through almost anything if we need to.

Imagine if you lose your laptop and everything is destroyed. You are locked out of all your bank accounts, social media as well as all your files. Does this "destroy"

your life? How crazy would an alien see this situation?
You can rebuild your wealth if you needed to as what you
have figured out until this far has taken you so far.
Just remember to take care of your mental health as that is
going to have a strong ability to create your financial
wealth.

46.   Conclusion

I started by stating that I have had the privilege of hanging around with and getting to know some of the richest people in the world. Yes, many of them inherited their wealth. Simply because your parents had money, they got you into the right golf course so you could connect with the wealthy and those wealthy people then ended up becoming investors in your business and helping you with further contacts.

But a big part of wealth creation is things like self-confidence and skills. You don't need to go to the most expensive schools to get this – you can develop these on your own.

In this era things have become cheaper than at any other point in history. For instance, I can easily move out of my expensive home in London to a much cheaper apartment in Peshawar, Pakistan and continue to do most of the work that I need to get done. I could get my expenses down to under USD 1,000 per month.

You don't need to own a house to feel rich. In fact most people take on a substantial loan to be able to pay for that house. Depending on where you live you likely don't need a car either. The wealthier cities of the world like London and New York in fact now encourage their citizens to use bicycles as a form of transportation.

My point is that you need to understand that if you had a billion dollars, your life wouldn't be much different than if you had a million dollars. In fact if anything you would have more responsibility to help the world if you had a billion dollars.

You can achieve your financial goals if that is what is a priority to you. As I live in London, I am seeing seminars all the time on people teaching about wealth creation. The nice thing for me to see is even in a country like Pakistan influencers like Rehan Allahwala, Azad Chaiwala, Sunny Ali, Hisham Sarwar and Shakeel Ahmad Meer teaching about wealth creation through Facebook and YouTube in the native language of Urdu. Platforms that one of the richest countries in the world, the United States, has provided to be used in almost all the poorest countries in the world.

As I write this sentence, I am 45 years old. I have the best life and that is thanks to the Internet. I can listen to any song that I want at any time through my Spotify subscription which costs me USD 10 per month. I can watch hundreds of movies on NetFlix which also costs me USD 10 per month. I use a National Health Service app so that any medication I can get sent to me via the mail. I can use an App like UberEats or Gorrillas to send me groceries in under 15 minutes from when I order them.

I can work from my room which can be in almost any country in the world with an internet connection. Most of my knowledge I give away for free from books like this or my online courses that I sell on AmirAnzur.com.

You too can compete with me from almost anywhere that you are sitting. My goal is to create as much wealth as I can. In the words of Walt Disney "We don't make movies to make money. We make money to make more movies".

It is the same for me. I don't want money for moneys sake. To have a large number in a database in a bank account. Or to show off my car (I much rather use Uber than drive myself) or a big house (I like things simple and bigger house means more guests).

I make money so I can reinvest it into businesses that will help the world. I love coaching people to be more successful in their lives and businesses as well as love creating software for clients.

For me the Internet is like a canvas and creating businesses and brands is like creating a painting. I love being an Internet artist and that is my path to wealth creation. You could have your own path in property or stocks and shares or buying a Subway franchise. Get into something you will enjoy doing. Find a way to serve the world and you will get rewarded – eventually.

Remember that we are playing the game of capitalism. Sometimes you will be making more money than me and sometimes I will get ahead. It is not a linear line to wealth. We all have our ups and downs.

I know this book didn't give you all the answers and teach you that you need to do ABC in that order, and you will create wealth. Because if it was that easy, everyone would be doing it (and it would not be as much fun).

Instead, I have taught you that you need confidence to get started. You need to value your time so that you are creating as much value for the world as possible and that will get you the rewards. To enjoy the journey of wealth creation.

The United States became the richest country in the world as they promoted capitalism. The gamification of creating value in the world. That is why the greatest innovations come from the US including the TV, Radio, airplane, the personal computer, iPhone, Android etc. Even if you live in a country like Pakistan and capitalism isn't as appreciated as it is in the US, you can now start to compete especially if the products and services are digital and have no physical borders to cross.

Although you might have paid for this book, I encourage you to share it with friends and redistribute it so that we can create a wealthier world quicker. For some people, even paying a single cent or rupee brings in too many barriers to downloading or reading.

This is also a digital asset as now that you have gone through it, it means I have built up a relationship with you. These 25,000 words which should take you less than 3 hours to read means that you have heard me talking for 3 hours. That is a relationship and that has value. All this is virtual. All I needed was a virtual copy of Microsoft Word and I was able to create this virtual asset.

You too can do this. There is no scarce land that I had to buy to create this asset. There are no machines apart from my laptop that I needed to create this asset. Your asset could be software and that just means that you could teach yourself to code or hire someone on Upwork to do it for you. It could be a piece of writing or some advice. You can make money in several ways in the digital economy.

Don't just think of wealth as a number in the bank account. A good review you leave for a friend for his restaurants is a tiny bit of wealth you have created as she appreciates what you have done for her. You can leave a review on Amazon for this book for instance and in return I will "owe" you a small favour. I will appreciate it. You will have built a little relationship asset between you and I and that might someday turn into financial wealth.

The only thing that won't make you money is inaction. You can't learn to swim unless you jump in the water and do it. Pick a vehicle for wealth creation, learn as much as you can about it and then jump in. This also means understanding the meaning of "affordable loss" i.e., to invest what you can afford to lose.

The number of millionaires and billionaires that are being produced is only getting higher and higher. Wealth is not a zero-sum game. Go out and create yours – it doesn't mean you are taking it away from someone else. The only thing stopping you is your mindset.

If you would like to try making money through affiliate marketing you can visit AmirAnzur.com and learn how I can pay you up to 50 % commissions for helping me sell some of my own products and services

I wish you the best in your journey.

47.   How to Make Money Through This Book

In marketing, they teach you that you should have a call to action. So, here is the call to action for Wealthology and a chance for both of us to make money together.

Firstly, you could take some coaching from me for instance by joining the Wealthology Club. This club has a weekly meeting online as well as a monthly meetup in London or locally to you when we can find enough of a community around you.

Having a community of people that want to improve their life through wealth creation will mean that you reach your wealth goals faster.

The Wealthology Club starts at GBP 100 per month and you can quit at any time.

Besides from the Wealthology Club, I have many more bespoke products and services that you can check out on www.AmirAnzur.com

Secondly, you can become an affiliate of mine. This means that if you spread the word about me to someone that ends up buying my products and services, I will pay you up to 50 % of what they pay.

So, for instance, if they join the Wealthology Club you make GBP 50 per month, every month. If they stay with me for a year this could mean GBP 300 for you per referral.

You could sign up as an affiliate on www.AmirAnzur.com and get your unique affiliate link like www.AmirAnzur.com/1. If you forward that to a friend and they end up buying something from me, you end up with the referral credit.

Otherwise, they can also put in the "Where did you hear about us" field your email, number or social media profile and I will give you credit for the sale.

My highest coaching and consulting product sell for GBP 2,000,000 and the commission for this is GBP 1,000,000.

I know how difficult it is to sell and market and that is why I am outsourcing it to people like you. If you help me bring clients for my products and services, we both win.

You can do this by simply forwarding this book or my other books ("Pakonomics – Why Americans Earn 53 Times More Than Pakistanis and What To Do About That" or "Internetism – How to Create Wealth in the Internet Economy".

I am giving you an opportunity and you could ignore it or take a few hours out of your day to check out my website at www.AmirAnzur.com and see how we could both help each other.

If you have any questions, you can reach me through WhatsApp me at +447733003930 or amir@amiranzur.com.

Amir Anzur

aartec.com | AmirAnzur.com
amir@amiranzur.com
+447733003930
LinkedIn.com/in/AmirAnzur
facebook.com/AmirAnzur
instagram.com/AmirAnzur
YouTube.com/AmirAnzur
TikTok.com/@AmirAnzur | Twitter.com/AmirAnzur

This page is blank for you to write notes on the key things you learned from this book.

This page is blank for you to write notes on the key things you learned from this book.

Write out your "Why" of Why creating wealth is important in your life. Having a reason will help you achieve it.

Write out what you will do to accelerate your wealth creation journey.

What is something you can do right now to speed up your
wealth creation journey (e.g., checking out
www.AmirAnzur.com will be one action you can take!)

Printed in Great Britain
by Amazon